THE ART OF THE TRADE

THE ART OF THE TRADE

MASTERING THE ANALYTIC AND INTUITIVE ELEMENTS OF SUCCESSFUL TRADING

R. E. McMaster, Jr.

McGraw-Hill

New York   San Francisco   Washington, D.C.   Auckland   Bogotá
Caracas   Lisbon   London   Madrid   Mexico City   Milan
Montreal   New Delhi   San Juan   Singapore
Sydney   Tokyo   Toronto

Library of Congress Cataloging-in-Publication Data

McMaster, R. E.
    The art of the trade / by R. E. McMaster, Jr.
      p.   cm.
    ISBN 0-07-045542-2
    1. Portfolio management.   2. Investment analysis.   3. Stock exchanges.
  I. Title.
  HG4529.5.M39 1999
  332.6—dc21   98-37848
                                                                CIP

McGraw-Hill

*A Division of The **McGraw·Hill** Companies*

1 2 3 4 5 6 7 8 9 0   DOC/DOC   9 0 4 3 2 1 0 9

ISBN 0-07-045542-2

The sponsoring editor for this book was Stephen Isaacs, the editing supervisor was Penny Linskey, and the production supervisor was Suzanne Rapcavage. It was set in Fairfield by Carol Barnstable of Carol Graphics.

Printed and bound by R. R. Donnelley & Sons Company.

McGraw-Hill books are available at special quantity discounts to use as premiums and sales promotions, or for use in corporate training programs. For more information, please write to the Director of Special Sales, McGraw-Hill, 11 West 19th Street, New York, NY 10011. Or contact your local bookstore.

To my mentor, Richard Russell,
who persuaded me to trade
and write about the markets as my
primary occupation

CONTENTS

ACKNOWLEDGMENTS

The compelling task of organizing over 25 years of market insight into a meaningful and coordinated book would not have been possible without the faithful word processing, editing and constructive criticism of my diligent staff, Marie Lechow, Barbie Ott, and Nina Mourning. Through her thoughtful and insightful questions, Jayne Pearl helped to make this book more user friendly.

Market analysis is not an exact science—no, it's a small part science, but mostly it's an art. The crux of this "art" is in intuiting which items and indicators to believe at any given time and which items to "throw out."

RICHARD RUSSELL

Dow Theory Letters
July 29, 1998

THE ART OF THE TRADE

INTRODUCTION

The word *trade* in English usage is both a noun and a verb. As a noun, a trade is an individual's occupation, a calling, a job, what you do daily to earn a living in the economic arena of life. As a verb, to trade is to swap, barter, exchange goods and/or services, or in the context of this work, to buy and sell stocks, futures contracts, currencies, and options on the listed "trading" exchanges.

In reality, to trade (verb) consistently in a successful manner, you must approach "trading" as a trade (noun). Trading is not some cavalier, whimsical on-and-off affair. The art of trading is a trade (occupation). Whether your main profession is trading on exchanges, managing a business, or selling real estate, you must consider trading as a lifestyle, a trade. When you trade actively, you can trade securities or commodities on many exchanges. You don't have to specialize in stocks, bonds, currencies, or commodities, because they all trade pretty much the same way, technically speaking. You do need the skill and experience of understanding the way markets work, however.

In today's complex society, our trade (occupation) requires specialization and division of labor, but trading in markets requires just the opposite: integration of many skills, perspectives, and intuition. My unique approach to trading is holistic, integrating insight from diverse disciplines, such as science, mathematics, philosophy, religion, medicine and alternative medicine, psychotronics, and politics, as well as focused commodity and stock trading, investing, international currency management, and agricultural involvement.

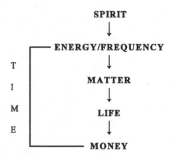

FIGURE I.1 The Integration of Reality

The premise of this book is that human knowledge is progressive. As we have developed a better understanding of ourselves from research in these many fields, we have more clues about our spiritual, mental, emotional, behavioral, and physical processes that we used to take for granted, that we were unconscious about, that we were simply intuitive with regard to, or that fell through the cracks and led to repeated cycles of error. This book synthesizes some of this new thinking so it can be integrated into the level of consciousness of traders, so they can be more aware synergistically of the factors they need to pull together, to have an opportunity to trade more successfully on a consistent basis.

As Figure I.1 shows, reality is the integration of spirit, energy/frequency, matter, life, and money. Spirit is living, conscious energy with personality, power, and purpose. It can manifest as energy/frequency, and when it slows down below the speed of light and sets up a standing electromagnetic field, it is transformed into matter. When you add to matter consciousness, awareness on various levels, it becomes life. (People, of course, have logic, emotion, will, ego, and self-awareness.) Money is stored evidence of the human spirit, energy, and accumulated life over time. When people die, the assets they leave behind are evidence of their stored spirit, matter, energy, life, and money. Their legacy reflects how they spent their lives. Energy, matter, life, and money all operate in the realm of time. Spirit is outside time but also permeates it. This is how the pieces of reality as we know it fit together.

Trading also inescapably involves money. In our late twentieth-century society, money has effectively become the measure of all things, especially success. Money is basic to our survival too. So, while *The Art of the Trade* is about making money, it considers much more—survival, status, and self-worth.

This book will also show you how to use both sides of your brain—a critical component of successful trading. The left side of the brain controls your verbal skills, focuses on details, and involves practical, concrete matters, orderly sequences, and your reactions to the physical world. It is noted for reasoning, mathematics, language, scientific skills, and logic. The right side of the brain is visual, spatial; it provides you with the overall picture. It is emotional and abstract, and deals with shapes and patterns. The right side of the brain is where the spiritual world interfaces. It is the region of your brain from which your imagination, creativity, art, insight, and intuition spring forth.

Any time you trade, you have subjective perceptions regarding the future. You are operating in an environment of uncertainty, investing in the unknown where there is limited and imperfect information. You must balance the intuitive insights of the right brain (traditionally called feminine) with the analytical work of the left brain (traditionally called masculine). In Eastern terms, the yang (left brain) must lead, ground, catalyze, and integrate with the yin (right brain). The conscious must illuminate the subconscious. The analytical (left brain) must provide a grounding foundation from which intuitive and creative energy (right brain) can emerge. This is why trading is an art, not an exact science.

It is no accident that many of the consistently successful, qualified analysts and traders are musicians. W. D. Gann, a renowned trader from the first half of the twentieth century, was a serious student of music. He saw the similarities between the harmonics of his era and the ebbs and flows of the market. Gilbert Kaplan, former publisher and editor of *Institutional Investor* magazine, has conducted the London Symphony Orchestra and even has cut several CDs. I find that playing the piano helps integrate both sides of my brain. Music is not only creative and artistic; it also draws on science and mathematics, thus utilizing both sides of the brain.

As I learned the hard way, making and keeping money has little to do with money itself. Rather, making and keeping money is a function, or by-product, of playing the trading game correctly and consistently. To do this, you must have a rich reserve of psychological capital, and an integrated left and right brain, in addition, of course, to financial capital. I have seen far too many traders burn out like shooting stars, burn up their psychological capital, lose their ability to trade successfully, lose their money, and even die prematurely, because of lack of balance in their lives. They did not understand that trading is an art as well as a science. They did not integrate the analytical (left brain/yang) and intuitive (right brain/yin) elements of successful trading. They did not balance their psychological capital with financial capital.

This book will help you maintain your emotional and mental reserves—which I call psychological capital—in order to preserve and increase your financial capital. In fact, your most important capital is not money; it is your psychological capital, which empowers you to trade to make money. Without it, you will not be able to preserve or increase your financial capital for long. (And, of course, good health supports your psychological capital. "You're not wealthy unless you're healthy.")

Your psychological capital reserves depend upon the degree to which you manage stress in your personal and professional life. Just as athletes need downtime between races to run successfully, traders need downtime to recharge so they can mentally freewheel and be refreshed to reengage the markets. Floor traders who go from opening bell to closing bell, trying to squeeze every penny possible out of every trade, day after day and week after week without taking a break, are bound to burn out quickly. I'd say the majority—perhaps 80 percent—are like that. This is why many floor traders are in their twenties or early thirties. When you deplete your psychological capital, you become blinded in your ability to discern the markets. You lose the fine edge that is often the difference between success and failure.

I learned this lesson firsthand. I began trading in the early 1970s, when I was a young second lieutenant in the U.S. Air Force, a few years before my first son was born. I worked my way up to perhaps two or three trades a day and within a few years was able to make fairly consistent profits. In 1979, when my son was six, he developed a severe form of epilepsy. Doctors did not expect him to live; and if he did, they told my wife and me that he would likely need to be institutionalized. I spent the next 13 years investigating every possible accommodation, medication, and alternative medical approach, never knowing when a seizure would strike. He was in the unlucky 5 percent for whom normal epilepsy medication was ineffective. But my long and tedious, heart-wrenching efforts paid off. Today he is married and basically lives a normal life. But at the time, the stress in my personal life wreaked havoc on my ability to trade effectively. I cut back my personal trading activity to about two or three trades a week and my personal profits plummeted by almost 50 percent.

Back in 1971, my very first investments consisted of a few hundred dollars of junk silver coins and some South African gold-mining stocks. Then, in 1973, I traded my first contracts in the futures markets—OJ and lumber—very difficult markets to trade because the volume and open interest are so low. I didn't know any better. However, some luck enabled me to profit to the tune of more than $1000 per contract in orange juice and lumber futures. I said to myself, "Wow! This is fun and easy." But it wasn't long before the sad truth settled in. It took a great deal of work to learn *The Art of the Trade*. I was not able to break even consistently for another three years, long before my son became ill. And it took several more years before I felt I was consistent, confident, competent, and comfortable trading. The effort was equivalent to the energy I spent on my undergraduate and master's studies combined, and appropriately it took almost the same amount of time.

That time and energy were well spent, however. Knowing how to trade is a skill I would not exchange for anything in the world. It has provided me with the ability to earn a living in any market, anywhere. Whether you're trading Japanese yen on the SIMEX in Singapore, or any other security or commodity or currency on any of more than 50 exchanges around the world, the technical patterns and rules for successful trading are basically the same.

> The market will find every hole in your personal and professional armor.

Trading can be invaluable in providing insights for dealing with the personal and professional issues that all of us face in life. The trading life cycles of the markets are a microcosm of your own life cycle. As you trade and learn about the market and how it oscillates, you see many parallels to what you experience in your own life and business. The only difference is that futures market contracts have shorter life spans, like a compressed holographic view of life.

Trading has helped me learn a great deal about my own strengths, weaknesses, biases, fears, and hopes. It has helped me become "street smart" more quickly than I would have otherwise become. For example, the markets don't allow you the time to live with your illusions. People can survive for many years with their illusions, doing things incorrectly, imprecisely, or inefficiently, but that is not so in the market. You can be successful in business by riding a primary trend like the computer industry without dealing with your personal issues. But the market demands that you deal with your personal issues, in part because of the emotional charge attached to money. The market will find every hole in your personal or professional armor.

I have learned to be more patient, admit when I am wrong, cut my losses short, let my profits ride, be more precise, attentive, effective, efficient, and focused. Trading the markets successfully has forced me to become more professional and to get my act together personally. Another important lesson from trading that I apply to my life is that if a certain action works out, I stay with it. If it doesn't, I get out. "Going with the flow" in life is the same thing as "trading with the trend" in a market. Most important, I have learned that there is very little in my life that I can control. I can only do the best I can, and be content with that.

Many traders are looking for the Holy Grail in one computerized technical system or another. In 1978, as one of E. F. Hutton's nationally approved commodities trading advisers

(CTAs), I helped develop the first computerized trading program used nationally to trade commodity futures contracts. As a pioneer, I have learned there is no Holy Grail. There is only the hard work of left-brain analysis that allows the creative and intuitive right brain to kick in, creating *The Art of the Trade*.

HOW TRADING IS AND IS NOT LIKE GAMBLING

There is a misconception in financial circles these days that trading—particularly futures trading—is like gambling and totally different from investing. The key, of course, is not to be an amateur player, either as a gambler or as a trader. And although learning *The Art of the Trade* will vastly improve the odds of consistent successful trading, there actually are some similarities and lessons to be gleaned from successful professional gamblers.

First, though, let's distinguish between traders and investors. Trading is a subset of investing. Investors buy and sell for the long term. They look for stocks that are undervalued, for example, and hold these investments for appreciation and dividends. On the other hand, traders look for opportunities to profit in the market. They may buy the same securities that investors buy, but they normally won't hold them as long. An investor, for example, may buy and hold Microsoft for three years, whereas a trader may be in and out of Microsoft two dozen or more times in three years. Also, investors do not, as a rule, sell short. Traders will sell a market short, looking to profit as prices fall. For example, if the Japanese recession causes Japan to cancel huge orders of wheat, a trader might ride that trend down in wheat futures contracts by selling it short. When the wheat futures market gets way oversold, however, the trader may turn around and buy wheat for a rebound, for the trade. That's something an investor would never do. An investor would sit on the sidelines in a bear market and wait to buy wheat to hold for the long term.

Here's another example of the difference between a trader and an investor. Picture two people at a garage sale who spot antiques they believe are undervalued. The trader will buy the antiques, fix them up, and sell them a few weeks later. The investor will buy them and hold them indefinitely.

Now let's compare trading and gambling. A trader is not like a reckless gambler who blows $10,000 over a wild weekend in Las Vegas, nor is a trader akin to someone who buys five $1 raffle tickets in hopes of winning the state lottery. Neither of these casual, recreational gambling activities requires any work, planning, forethought, or execution. Traders, on the other hand, do have much in common with professional gamblers, who treat gambling as a business. In gambling, the odds are always in the house's favor. Professional gamblers know how to work those odds, much as professional traders look for and find opportunities that less seasoned traders miss. And, just as in the Old South there are many ways to skin a cat (fish), so there are many ways to gamble successfully, and many successful approaches to trading. One of the most successful traders I know is so skillful at computing odds that when he goes to Las Vegas, the casinos pay him *not* to gamble by furnishing him with complimentary limos, rooms, meals, and tickets to the shows.

Trading and gambling have other things in common. First, they involve putting money on the line in an arena of uncertainty. Just as gamblers don't know how the dice are going to roll or how the cards will fall, traders cannot predict how prices will fluctuate. The difference is that in trading the odds are not stacked against you with actuarial certainty, as they are in gambling.

Second, both require hard work, calculating where the probabilities of greatest return exist. Let's face it, the only sure thing in life is death (and some would say taxes). When you trade or gamble professionally, you can only predict the probable outcome.

Third, to be successful, traders and professional gamblers must exercise good money management, or allocation of financial resources. Professional gamblers will allocate how much capital they're willing to risk. They will take to the tables only what they're willing to lose. Traders, on the other hand, must allocate personal financial assets in three steps. First, they must decide how much capital they're willing to trade with in their account. Then they must decide how much they're willing to trade in any particular market sector. Last, they must break that down to how much they're willing to risk in any individual trade.

Traders can learn much from the rules of successful gambling, where the odds are stacked against the player and the pressure is intense. Fighter aircraft pilots refine their skills in impossibly difficult training circumstances, so that when they engage a real-life challenge, combat proves less difficult than what they experienced in training. This gives them an edge in coping successfully. Similarly, by studying how professional gamblers operate in their intense arenas, traders can be better prepared for their own challenging circumstances. So here are the common principles that apply to both occupations.

DON'T PLAY A GAME THAT YOU DON'T UNDERSTAND

Successful gamblers avoid games where they can't figure the odds, don't know the ins and outs, are awkward or uncomfortable, or can't be totally professional. Traders also need to have a professional working knowledge of the arena in which they are trading as well as the item that they're trading. This takes time. Don't be fooled by "beginner's luck," which invariably gives way to "paying your dues." Traders have to become seasoned by experience, which teaches the intricacies and nuances, the small but very critical details, of what they're trading as well as the trading arena. The old trading rule, "When in doubt, stay out," applies.

If you can't stay out, try piggybacking another trader. Perhaps a family member or friend is a seasoned trader who would be willing to mentor you in exchange for your doing some research and technical work. By and large, most people learn from books and seminars, which are valuable. But there's no substitute for being able to work alongside an experienced trader who understands what is going on, has done it successfully, and can be trusted. Money can be made by following successful, expert traders and doing exactly what they say to do, when they say to do it. Just as in any other area of life, you have to learn the ropes in trading. The value of an apprenticeship must not be discounted.

Why would the pros be willing to share their secrets? For one thing, the markets are huge, and there is considerable liquidity. Next, it won't affect their position or odds if an understudy piggybacks their transactions in a small way. What's more, novices can be equally valuable for the pros as sources of emotional support. Mentors may enjoy talking about what they're thinking. They may also become more focused. Traders tend to perform more professionally when they have someone looking over their shoulder. They are less likely to give into their weaknesses, biases, and vulnerabilities, because they want to set a good example. For instance, when my son is shadowing me, I am more careful to follow my own trading rules precisely, particularly when his own money is on the line.

AVOID GAMES WHERE THE ODDS ARE NOT IN YOUR FAVOR

Professional gamblers stay out of games where the deck is stacked so to speak, and the "house" has a considerable advantage, as in the case of one-armed bandits (slot machines). Blackjack at least requires playing skill and has better odds. Successful traders will likewise avoid a trade where the risk/reward ratio is unfavorable. They will pass on it. Trades are like buses. One comes along frequently. Good traders must wait for high-probability trades where the risk/reward probabilities are heavily in their favor. For me, this means at least 3-to-1 odds—the odds of a gain being three times greater than the odds of a loss, the profit potential being three times greater than the loss potential.

For instance, say December silver is trading at $4.40 to $4. 50 per ounce for several months, and all of a sudden it breaks out on the upside to $4.55 with increasing volume and open interest. Many people who use moving averages and professional funds that utilize trend-following trading systems will move into December silver with the technical breakout market buy signal. Using books such as *Technical Analysis of Stock Trends,* by Robert D. Edwards and John F. Magee (AMACOM Books, 1997), you can even compute the odds that a move to $4.80 will have, say, an 80 percent chance of occurring. So the odds are well in your favor of a 30-cent profit in silver versus a 10-cent loss if you put your protective stop loss at $4.40, once December silver rallies above $4.50. Actually, the revised probabilities in your favor are 12 to 1 ($.8 \times 30$ cents = 24; $.2 \times 10$ cents = 2; $24 \div 2 = 12$).

You can compute probabilities of different outcomes by finding similar patterns (in this case, the breakout of a trading range) in all kinds of markets—stocks, commodities, currencies, bonds—through history. Those patterns tend to repeat because technical setups reflect human nature, which is fairly predictable.

SHOP FOR THE BEST BUSINESS OPPORTUNITY

In Las Vegas, different casinos have different payoffs, some higher, some lower, for the same game of chance. So, too, there are many variables a trader needs to consider concerning the selection of an exchange and particularly a broker.

Different exchanges have different rules and customs, particularly abroad. Before you trade in a market that is new to you, make sure you understand its ways, its trading hours, margin requirements, limits on the size of trades, how orders are executed, and whether there is a way to verify that your order is executed properly. Look beyond the "killing" you think you can make in a market to take care of important details. On closer inspection, for instance, you may find the margins are too high or the trading hours are inconvenient.

Despite the growing interest in trading via the Internet, I still prefer working with a broker. Executions via the Internet are slower than going through a brokerage firm. Also, I like the idea of having someone else verify what I'm doing, to make sure I am on course, much as a navigator helps a pilot fly to a given destination. But you need to look for the right broker, one who will meet your individual trading requirements professionally and who is compatible personally. Commissions are important, but also look at what services you will receive for your money. Do you want a broker who will do research for you, who will alert you when a stock or commodity price changes, who will be helpful and supportive? Or would you prefer someone who'll just execute your orders? How much and what kind of assistance do you need? If you need a great deal, then don't expect to pay the lowest commissions. But if you don't need a great deal of backup support, there's no point paying for a high-priced broker who offers extraneous services.

I look for a broker who exercises professional attention to detail. Rapport is also important. Life is too short to go through it with people who are cold and cynical or unsupportive. So when I check out brokers, I look not only at their professional track record, but also at their personal life, to the degree they are willing to share it. I could not care less where they went to school, but I do want to know if they come from hardworking, honest families, if they worked their way through college, what jobs they've held before and for how long. In short, I want to know my broker's character, work ethic, and job history.

Because deals over the phone are made with a verbal handshake, I believe it's critical to check out the character of the brokers you are considering. Do they have integrity? Do they have a heart to serve? Is too much ego involved—will they become jealous if you make a lot of money? Are they snide or sarcastic or begrudging about orders you place? Are they moody? Do they seem to spend more time churning commissions, making themselves rich, or are they happy to help you do the best you can?

I ask candidly about the basis of a broker's values and ethics. I like to work with someone who has some sort of spiritual or religious base. I usually ask for three references from present clients. It's important to me that we develop a "team" mentality. Fulfilling these needs contributes to my bottom-line return. I also like to work with an established brokerage firm—one that's been around for at least a decade and that has a solid financial statement and reputation. I check to see that the firm uses a reputable clearinghouse, one that has been in business for some time.

DON'T BUY OR BET MORE THAN YOU CAN AFFORD TO LOSE

Another key requirement for long-term success as a trader, as it is for a gambler, is sustainability—the ability to stay in the trade or the game. You have to be able to stay with it until things turn your way, which is a function of preserving three things:

- *Psychological capital.* Don't let sudden losses scare you (fear) or sudden wins influence you (greed) away from your trading and money management strategies.
- *Physical capital.* Just as a gambler cannot stay at the table for 24 hours, so a trader needs time out. Make sure you replenish yourself by eating, sleeping, and exercising adequately.
- *Financial capital.* Whether you are winning or losing, stick with your original money management plan. Nothing distorts judgment more than having a larger position on the line, either gambling or trading, than you can afford to lose. If you do, you may get out of the trade too soon if it's moving in your favor or stay in the trade, particularly holding onto a loss, for too long.

TRADE WITH THE TREND

Good gamblers increase their bet when they're winning, and reduce it when they're losing. If you have had several losses in a row, you should consider reducing the number of shares or futures contracts that you purchase and reevaluate what you are doing. At the very minimum, do not increase your bets when you're losing. Averaging down is usually fatal. One of the major principles of good money management is to cut your losses short.

I cannot emphasize too strongly that when prices are declining, you should not scale-down buy or average in. Say you hold one contract of silver long and prices start moving lower. In scale-down buying, you would buy more silver as the price continued to sink, hoping that you will make a bigger gain when (or if) the price of silver bounces back up. It may work. But if the bottom keeps dropping out of silver, you end up with a huge loss in one trade that will destroy all your hard work and hard-earned money.

Similarly, when prices are trending up, scaling in short sales is equally dangerous. For example, if you sold a contract of silver short and the price continued to rise, by scaling up short sales, you would decide to add to your short position in silver in the hope that silver prices will fall by the time you offset your short sale, or receive a delivery notice.

A critical trading rule is to cut your losses short and let your profits ride. Sure enough, it may take a while to recognize when things are going sour. You must watch carefully for when a market starts to change trend. One of my rules is that if you have to work too hard to make something work—whether it's a relationship, a business deal, or a trade—it usually is not going to work. In addition, sometimes we're on and sometimes we're not, on a day-to-day basis, just as your golf game is sometimes superb and at other times it stinks.

When you are having a great winning streak, that's not the time to take a month's vacation or go fishing. When you're on as a swing trader, and the distractions in your personal and professional life are at a minimum, that's the time to stay in the game and continue to trade. Just stick to your trading system and money management criteria.

FOCUS ON PLAYING THE GAME CORRECTLY AND MAKING MONEY WILL TAKE CARE OF ITSELF

Good gamblers forget that they're playing for money. They simply focus on executing their gambling system. Making money is a by-product of doing things correctly. Good gamblers analyze their chances of winning or losing according to the odds, and then take a position. They focus on the task at hand. Focusing on the money on the table (or in the trade) is a destructive distraction that inhibits gambling performance and trading success. Making money is a by-product of having traded correctly by sticking to and executing a trading and money management system successfully.

Instead of harping on the amount of money you have at stake in the market, focus instead on:

• The markets themselves—looking for trading opportunities
• Your trading systems
• Other helpful information
• Money management
• Yourself

Thinking too much about the money that you're trading with, rather than about playing the game correctly—whether you win or lose—will inescapably short-circuit your ability to make correct trading decisions. Gambling and trading both require concentration, which you cannot effectively maintain when you start to focus on the money involved. A good gambler decides whether a bet is worth making in terms of the probability of winning. A good trader is best served by computing whether the possible return on a trade is worth the risk. Neither professional gamblers nor traders are distracted when the stakes get high; they don't get cold feet and fold just because they've had a huge, unexpected winning or losing streak.

REMEMBER THAT THE MONEY IN A POSITION IS REAL MONEY

This is not a contradiction to the previous point, but it certainly poses a paradox. When gamblers or traders have a series of significant wins, they tend to get sloppy executing their system because their gains feel like free money, or the house's or the market's money. It's not. It's their money—real money, hard-earned gains. As explained in greater depth in Chapter 2, when traders forget this, they lose touch with reality. They get caught up in the "game" of trading. Carelessness has a way of dissipating hard-earned profits. Easy wins or a series of wins make traders more flippant and reckless, and willing to take wild chances.

Once again, the trick is simply to stick with your trading and money management systems. So the paradox here is that while you're trading, forget about the money and just focus on playing the game and trading correctly; let the money take care of itself. On the other hand, in the face of wins or losses, remember this *is* your money, real money. By sticking to your strategy for your money, you will resist the temptation to take risks or be sloppy with what you might feel is the market's money.

PLAY AGGRESSIVELY, ESPECIALLY WHEN YOU ARE WINNING

How many times have you seen a winning football team or basketball team decide late in the game to "sit" on a lead? What normally happens? The players become conservative and risk-averse, and as a result their lead erodes. It's not that they become lazy; they become fearful, too conservative, and lose their focus and intensity. What got them the lead in the first place was aggressive play, taking risks, playing hard, and being courageous. As a result of becoming conservative and less aggressive, the opposing team tends to close the gap and make the game much closer than if the team in the lead had continued to play hard and to implement the strategy that helped it achieve the lead in the first place.

In a similar manner, traders on a winning streak may decide to take a smaller profit this time around. As mentioned above, they are focusing on the money, not on playing the game correctly. They become convinced that their "luck" can't go on forever. Instead of letting the market play itself out naturally, they become fearful that the market will turn against them. That's trading on emotion, not on a system.

Whether you've had five losses in a row, are suffering a hangover from the night before, or have a fishing trip planned, if your trading system signals a market entry, it's the right time to make a trade. A timid, complacent, or erratic trader will pass on the trade that the system has picked. This violates the principle of consistency.

Initiative in life pays off. You should continue to look aggressively for trades that meet your trading criteria. Being timid doesn't work. Big-money opportunities are lost when you violate the laws of probability by skipping a trade. Just like a gambler on a winning streak, you should aggressively trade with the trend when you're "on." The trend of winning trades will increase your equity, your financial capital.

Good professional gamblers or traders cannot feel like losers or else they'll likely play like losers. But neither gamblers nor traders should let a loss lead needlessly to further losses. Neither can afford to become reckless. A trap door to failure for both traders and gamblers is the tendency to try to make up for losses as soon as possible. When you lose, you may feel that the market or the casino has "your" money, that it owes your money back to you. You want it back and the game can become an emotional vendetta. In truth, the probabilities at a casino are completely objective; they are set mechanically. There is nothing emotional about the situations you face in trading either. The market just exists. It doesn't care if you win or lose. So trying to fit an emotional template on an environment that is oblivious to your emotional state is akin to standing in the ocean all night trying to stop the tide from rolling in. You'll lose. You may become angry, fight, feel that the market owes you something it doesn't, trade too heavily, and/or get angry at your broker. All the while, you are completely distracted from your primary comprehensive trading strategy. You must be willing to deal with the reality of your losses, assess them, learn from them, adjust your trading plan if necessary, and then move on.

STUDY THE "LAY OF THE LAND" BEFORE YOU TRADE

When professional gamblers first come to town, they will survey the casinos and the house rules, ascertain the odds, and check out the way the other players are playing before they ever sit down at a table and put their money on the line.

In the same way, you should be patient and implement all aspects of your trading strategy in a professional way before trading. You should paper-trade on different exchanges, in various markets, with different types of trades for a while, before putting your money on the line. It's like trying on a new dress or suit (once you've chosen a good clothing store) before you buy it. You want to make sure it feels good and fits before you make the purchase.

When I first started out, I looked at short-term day trading, where you jump in and out of the market 10 to 20 times a day. I didn't like it because I found it too hectic and emotionally draining; also it forced me to devote too much focus on a small number of markets. I didn't like using a long-term moving-average approach either, even though that's one of the best systems for following trends. Using moving averages, you may get hit with large initial losses when you're wrong. What worked best for me was surveying a number of markets, getting an overview, and then looking for markets that had technical setups with a risk/reward multiple between 1.5 and 3. This is more of a swing-trading approach. I traded on paper for six months before I traded my first futures contract.

You don't need to spend that much time on a day-to-day basis to become a professional trader. Numerous software programs—which you can find advertised in magazines such as *Futures* and *Technical Analysis of Stocks and Commodities,* or in

Investor's Business Daily—can help you try out different trading approaches before you risk a dime in the market.

Once you get the lay of the land, you can remain cool, calm, and collected in the face of market volatility. This will enhance your long-term probability of succeeding in the stock, bond, futures, metals, or currency markets. Easier said than done? You don't need to overhaul your personality; you just need to find a compatible system. You need to do your homework to develop a feel for what you're trading, the environment in which you're trading, the market you're trading, and the other players trading. It takes a while to settle in and gain a sense of what makes the market tick, the trend of the market.

Trading changes your response to situations, from being emotionally based to steeped in discipline. It enables you to avoid panicking in high-stress situations. Gamblers and traders who "like the action," and jump in before they've calmly assessed their environment, usually lose. Subjectivity and high emotion do not pay off in the long term. Doing your homework does.

TRADE ON INTUITION, NOT IMPULSE

Impulsive gamblers and traders usually lose. Traders who trade on impulse are usually ungrounded, very excitable, emotional, and often wrong about their trading decisions. Impulsive gamblers or traders tend to get carried away by greed and fear. This is in sharp contrast to the traders who study the markets over a long period of time. If you do your homework, you will develop a sense of intuition regarding the market. Intuition evolves from a foundation of long hours of study and work. It wells up from a long period of successful experience, thoughtful research, reflection, and wrestling with ideas, concepts, and markets.

It's like shopping for a suit by closing your eyes and pointing to one arbitrarily, as opposed to checking out several designs—the lines, the stitching, and where they were made—and then walking around the aisles once or twice before deciding which one to buy.

TAKE REGULAR BREAKS

Trading for too long tends to result in bad decisions. Just as the gambling casinos never close, today's financial markets have unlimited hours. Many go on for 24 hours day after day, month after month, year after year. Human beings can't hold up against such a juggernaut. You need rest so you don't wear out and break down. Otherwise, you will short-circuit mentally, emotionally, psychologically, and physically. You need time away from the markets to recharge your batteries, refresh your energies, study, learn new trading skills, contemplate the markets, and generally regroup.

If you burn up your psychological capital, you are sure to make costly trading mistakes. Everyone is different. How long you can go without a break depends on how much personal and professional stress you are juggling and how actively you are trading; it also depends on your mental mind-set, your emotional makeup, and your physical condition. One of my clients can trade 24 hours a day for three days when the markets are really hopping. Then he'll take an entire week off when the markets cool down or fortune moves against him.

I usually trade five days a week, from about 7:00 a.m. to 1:30 p.m. Mountain Time. I still follow the markets while I'm researching and writing my investment newsletter, *The Reaper,* and doing Cycle III, my trading hotline's recording of daily buy-and-sell recommendations. At night, I monitor what is happening overseas. I replenish my energy and focus by taking frequent three-day weekends, and getting away for at least a couple of weeks each year. It takes me 72 hours to unwind, and another 10 days or so of downtime to truly renew myself.

DO NOT BE INTIMIDATED BY SEEMINGLY INFALLIBLE TECHNOLOGY

Just as dealers in Las Vegas occasionally make mistakes at the casino tables, brokers can make mistakes in executing trades. Computers, too, are only as good as those who build them, operate them, and maintain them. You must be responsible and take the initiative to ensure that you execute trades and handle money forthrightly, expeditiously, honestly, and accurately.

At a minimum, I suggest that you monitor your monthly statements from your brokerage firm. Make sure excess funds are put in interest-bearing investments, such as Treasury bills. Balance the statement the same way you balance your checkbook. Make sure commissions, your market entries and exits, and the prices of those entries and exits match your notes and records.

Each day, double-check with your broker that your orders were filled—that futures contracts or shares of stock were purchased or sold at the appropriate time and price. You want to make sure your orders are carried out expeditiously. Check the market's "time and sales" through services such as CQG, Inc. (out of Glenwood Springs, Colorado) and Bloomberg (out of Princeton, New Jersey), which provide terminals with up-to-the-second quotes of trading markets. Let brokers know whether their executions are consistent with the prices you expected at the time you placed your orders. The very act of checking keeps brokers on their toes. You're making sure they are giving you the best executions and service they possibly can.

DON'T RELY ON SUPERSTITIOUS HABITS

Gamblers or traders who allow superstition to seriously influence their trading methodology will find their performance becoming unstable and erratic.

People often search for security and perfect knowledge when they're dealing with the unknown, particularly when it comes to such an emotional subject as money. Some trade only when their horoscope is favorable; others will buy wheat only on the full moon and sell it on the new moon. Some have lucky coins, rabbit's feet, worry beads, necklaces, or special jackets or ties. Some of these superstitions may seem innocuous, but they are not. The subconscious is very powerful. When people believe they need some object or circumstance to trade successfully, superstition tends to become a self-fulfilling prophecy. If you can't find your lucky tie, for example, you may find a way to self-destruct your trades that day. It's simply dangerous to rely on something external to you as a source of your faith and ability to trade.

Superstition provides a "handle" that some traders grab in an attempt to increase their power in trading. But using superstition in trading is akin to relying upon quicksand as a foundation. A much better approach is simply to follow the primary trend in trading and let the "trend be your friend." Using a combination of fundamental, technical, psychological, and timing analysis as a basis for making trading decisions will provide much better results.

It is important to create a comfort zone in which to trade. I find I'm too distracted to trade if my desk is cluttered, or if there's a lot of noise (chaos) in my environment. I'll just pass on trading then, because I'm usually not able to make as good decisions as when my environment is peaceful. This is not a superstition as such; it's a structure I know I need to have to function fully. It's important to find things that are not in the realm of superstition to make your environment as user-friendly as possible, to help you function at your maximum trading capability.

One way to distinguish between superstition and a comfort zone is to ask yourself whether the practice can be scientifically validated as positively contributing to your ability to function effectively. Some traders believe they need a certain kind of breakfast before they trade. That's okay. Maybe they're giving their bodies exactly what they need to help their brains function well.

If you identify a superstitious habit, you may find it difficult to wean yourself away from it. You don't have to go cold turkey, though. You can use your money management system for help. For instance, decide you will risk a certain amount of capital on nonsuperstitious trading. As you experience success with these trades and gain confidence in your ability to make good trades without your superstitious practices, you should steadily increase the amount of capital you trade in a nonsuperstitious way.

HARNESS AND INTEGRATE ALL YOUR MENTAL FACULTIES

You must have your wits about you. The best traders are in top shape spiritually, mentally, psychologically, emotionally, and physically. This does not allow for the debilitating use of drugs or alcohol, overeating, or even a sedentary lifestyle. Coping with stress successfully requires taking time off to relax (as mentioned above), and participating in other enjoyable activities. In other words, a long-term, balanced lifestyle is necessary for successful trading.

Trading is mental, indoors, sedentary, and stressful. So I try to balance it off by selecting hobbies that are nonmental, outside, active, and nonstressful: such as mountain biking, hiking, and skiing. I also find it is imperative to take downtime, to support significant others in my life, to read outside the markets, to grow spiritually, and to seek recreation that will bring joy and laughter to my life. Taking quiet time for spiritual reflection charges up my creative, freewheeling batteries. Don't forget to set aside time for research, growth, and improving your skills in the markets too.

PRESERVE CAPITAL—BE WILLING TO BREAK EVEN

Look at it this way: If you lose half your trading capital, you have to make 100 percent on your money in order to get it all back. This suggests that even if you need to take partial profits in a position in order to break even for the remainder of the trade, you've adopted a solid, capital-preserving approach. First and foremost is preservation of capital. You may want to take partial short-term profits and let remaining positions ride. You may want to move as quickly as possible to a no-risk, breakeven situation.

For instance, if you have a "springboard" setup, in which the market has a high probability of moving sharply in a certain direction for a few days, often the market initially will move in your favor. When that occurs, if you're trading several futures contracts, you may want to take down a third or half of them on this initial rally. This allows you emotionally to better ride the trend with the rest of your trade. It's a good money management tool because it helps you move quickly to break even. By taking partial profits, you are in a net win situation. If the market then moves against you, hopefully the remaining positions will be stopped out at breakeven or a small loss and you'll still have a net win from taking partial profits earlier.

This is great psychological support too. It enables you to better ride the trend, but not with your full position, so you can have some banked profits too. How much should you pull down and how much of your position should you let ride in the market? Sell down to your own "sleeping" level—hold a position that is not so big that you can't sleep with it. Say, for instance, you have a springboard setup in stock index futures, and a quick momentum move gives you a $5000 open profit in a couple days on a couple of contracts. You might want to sell half your position (one contract) so that if the market gets volatile and moves against you, you won't lose all your profit. That will make it easier emotionally for you to let the rest of your position (one contract) ride with the market. The trade-off is you won't win as much if the market continues to move as originally projected.

Once you've started to trade astutely, one of the most important rules is to stay in the game. The longer you can hang in there, even during tough markets, the better your chances will be that you will eventually hit some trades that give you a big jump up in equity. My own history of trading shows that I tend to chop around sideways for a while, then have a huge run-up from a series of wins, and then move sideways again for a while. The trick is not to have huge drawdowns during the choppy periods. It's no different from fishing. You have to keep your bait in the water until the fish start biting. While they're not biting, however, you want to make sure you don't lose all your bait or lures on the bottom or exhaust yourself, so when the fish do start biting, you have enough bait and energy left to catch them.

SWALLOW A HEALTHY DOSE OF HUMBLE PIE

Humility is the most important character trait for a gambler to bring to the gambling table and for a trader to bring to the market. Many great philosophers have argued that humility is the most important virtue in an individual. In *The Seven Habits of Highly Successful People* (Simon and Schuster, 1990), Stephen R. Covey says we should seek to understand before we are understood. In other words, listen and comprehend before you speak. This way you get more information and can respond more effectively. It's the same way with the markets. To become a successful trader, you must learn to "listen to the market," to surrender to doing things correctly. Humility is the essence of being able to listen to what the market is doing, to really get in touch with it, and to respond to it wisely.

You need to abandon any arrogant, proud, or egotistical opinions of what you think the market will do. When you are entrenched in an opinion about the market, you are more likely to miss profitable moves, and less likely to stick to your trading and money management systems. Humility enables you to be responsive, while opinions corner you into a position or a specific market bias.

STAY WITH YOUR TRADING APPROACH

Gamblers tend to be afraid to take chances when they're losing and to be too aggressive when they're winning. Traders tend to ignore their trading philosophy and risk too little or pass on trades when they're losing. They tend to trade excessively with too much money or in too many positions when they're winning. "Wild traders may make it on Wall Street, but they rarely keep it," notes *Forbes* magazine columnist Kenneth L. Fisher in his book *One Hundred Minds That Make the Market* (Business Classics, 1994). The correct approach is to trade consistently, being cautious about cutting back too much when you're losing or adding on too much when you're winning.

PUTTING MONEY IN PERSPECTIVE

Money is basic to our very survival in the fractional-reserve, debt-based economic system in which we find ourselves today. But money is also very much a matter of the heart. We use money to measure our success and status, how we feel about ourselves. Basically, however, because we need money to put food on the table, our fear of not having enough money to feed our families can severely impact our psychological comfort zone.

They say there are three things that will ruin the best of us—money, sex, and power. Similarly, research done for years by the Sedona Institute in Arizona indicates there are three basic psychological needs that drive us—security, approval, and control—which are parallel to money, sex and power, only on a deeper level.

Your objective with regard to investing money is to make more of it—real money, not Monopoly money, not the market's money. When you invest, it is with real money that can purchase real goods and services. Often traders miss this basic perspective when they are in the markets, and so they lose focus. Many traders get wrapped up in wanting to be right. This desire to be right (correct) may lead them to take small profits instead of riding the trend of the market, and to let losses grow and grow instead of cutting losses short, and to pass up the next trading opportunity.

WHEN BEING RIGHT CAN GET YOU IN TROUBLE

Being right is not all it's cracked up to be. In fact, it can get you in deep trouble. I have yet to find anyone who wins on every trade, or even comes close to doing so. As Glen Ring noted in his newsletter *View of Futures,* "Losing trades are part of the business—a very necessary part." He explains that if being right were the most important factor of all, then taking a losing trade would be tantamount to admitting you were wrong about a market. You would have to hold a position until it became profitable. Sooner or later, the strain of the equity drawdown would bring you to your knees. So it's important to decide before you execute a trade the point at which you will consider yourself wrong on the trade and exit it. It can be a flat dollar amount (a money management stop), or it can be determined by market-generated signals such as a volatility trigger or a moving average. Or it can be a time stop, getting out after X number of days.

Look what failing to exit the market did to one trader. He decided that a market had gone "too high" and took a short position. The market then proceeded to lock up the allowable trading limit for three consecutive days. This put the trader on margin call. Instead of making plans to exit the market as soon as possible, he decided to ride the position out. Enough margin was dumped into the account to ride out 18 more limit moves. Sure enough, the market consumed all that capital. Those 18 limit moves did not come on a back-to-back basis; this trader had a few opportunities to minimize the loss. But even at one point when the position was just 10 limit moves behind, he kept his heels dug in and ended up taking a huge loss.

One way Ring recommends you can take the emotional sting out of being wrong is to think of trading in terms of probabilities: "By accepting there are high-probability and low-probability outcomes, your mind is more likely to be open to whatever happens." To my mind, the use of probabilities is the best way to handle the uncertainty of the market.

As Ring also points out, "Trading is not about being right or wrong. It is about making more money when you are right than you lose when you are wrong. . . . No matter how well you have done your work, there is only one entity in this business that is always right—the market."

Successful long-term traders must be comfortable with being correct only one-third of the time, which is about the average amount of time the market trends. One of the best ways to trade in a trending market is to use the moving-average approach. For instance, consider using the 3-, 9-, and 21-day moving averages, and waiting for crossover buy signals for entering and exiting the market when you want to go long. You could have a lot of whipsaws and losses from false crossover buy and sell signals, because the market trends only about a third of the time. But if you can live through those setbacks and not get emotionally attached to the fact that you'll be wrong about two-thirds of the time, then when the market does trend that one-third of the time, your gains will more than exceed the losses you take two-thirds of the time.

MAXIMIZING YOUR RETURNS

What about a reasonable rate of return? Historically, the real rate of return (interest rate minus inflation) has hovered at 2.5 to 3 percent. As Table 2.1 illustrates, although real interest rates have reached as high as 6.6 percent and as low as negative 2.3 percent during the past 30 years, the average has stayed in a narrower range of 1.8 and 2.6 percent.

In light of real interest rates, if you are making 15 percent to 30 percent, that is great. You are taking more risk and the payoff is higher. What if you're making 60 percent to 100 percent? In this case you have unusual talent, experience, commitment, and perhaps undeserved blessing, in addition to high risk. If your intensity is too high, you will likely burn up your psychological capital. Look at the average age of the floor traders on the commodity exchanges. They are primarily in their twenties and thirties. They have a tremendous amount of psychological capital to burn. You won't find many who are older, because they've burned out. Their psychological capital is exhausted.

TABLE 2.1   Managing Your Expectations about Reasonable
             Rates of Return

	Nominal Interest Rate (One-Year T-Bills)	Inflation (Consumer Price Index)	Real Interest Rate
1997	5.63	3.0	2.63
1996	5.52	3.3	2.22
1995	5.94	2.8	3.14
1994	5.32	2.6	2.72
1993	3.43	3.0	0.43
1992	3.89	3.0	0.89
1991	7.89	4.2	3.69
1990	5.86	5.4	0.46
1989	8.53	4.8	3.73
1988	7.65	4.1	3.55
1987	6.77	3.6	3.11
1986	6.45	1.9	4.55
1985	8.42	3.6	4.82
1984	10.91	4.3	6.61
1983	9.58	3.2	6.38
1982	12.27	6.2	6.02
1981	14.80	10.3	4.50
1980	12.00	13.5	-1.50
1979	10.65	11.3	-0.75
1978	8.34	7.6	0.74
1977	6.08	6.5	- 0.42
1976	5.88	5.8	0.08
1975	6.78	9.1	-2.32
1974	9.20	11.0	-1.80
1973	7.32	6.2	1.12
1972	4.95	3.2	1.75
1971	4.89	4.4	0.49
1970	6.90	5.7	1.20
1969	7.12	5.5	1.07
1968	5.69	4.2	1.49
1967	4.88	3.1	1.78

I look at returns on investments much the way I view hunting for a trophy buck. The odds of harvesting a trophy whitetail buck are less than 10 percent. The odds of harvesting a nice mature buck are 70 percent. I play the odds and harvest a mature buck—venison for our table, every year.

Yes, you can ride the big wave and look for the big killing in the market. But few people make a killing in the market—with one investment that makes them millionaires. Instead, I look for returns that will average anywhere from 15 percent to 30 per-

TABLE 2.2 The Rule of 72

Interest Rate (Percent)	Years to Double Your Money
5	14.4
6	12
7	10.3
8	9
9	8
10	7.2

cent a year. I am comfortable with that return because after I deposit my gains in my margin account, I know the compounding of interest effect will pay off in the long term.

If a client of mine has a $50,000 futures trading account, I recommend putting $40,000 in Treasury bills for use as original margin and leaving the other $10,000 for variability and drawdowns on any trading losses the client may incur. The client can then have his or her cake and eat it too. While the $40,000 serves as margin, it will also be earning compound interest.

The Rule of 72 tells you how long it takes compound interest to double the value of an investment. Table 2.2 shows that if you have an interest rate of 10 percent and you divide that into 72, your money will double in 7.2 years. Another example: If you deposit $10,000 in a 6 percent Treasury bond, it will take 12 years (72 ÷ 6 = 12) to grow to $20,000.

Compounding, making money slowly with patience, will help preserve your psychological capital in the long run and increase your longevity in the investing and trading marketplace. It will also give you peace of mind so you can make better trade selections and not be subject to many of the weaknesses (such as burnout) that wreck traders year in and year out. During the past 23 years that I have consulted with investors and traders, I have seen this wisdom prove itself over and over again in the real world of trading.

Keep in mind that you want to make money and keep it long term. If you do that, you will be able to compound your money. The compounding of money has been known historically as the "royal road to riches." It is a safe, secure road, and anyone can travel it. But it requires the discipline to save what you have earned, the perseverance to continue to invest this money wisely and safely, the intelligence to understand what you're doing and why, and the patience to let time and compound interest work for you.

In other words, your trading should be for the purpose of developing a capital pool of money that can grow safely on its own year in and year out and eventually free you from the necessity of trading. And incidentally, you will trade better when you no longer need to trade, when trading is more selective and simply fun. You want to trade like a millionaire who doesn't need the markets.

Compounding of interest may be a boring way to make money. But given time, it will make you rich. Just think: If you can make 10 percent on your money year after year, that money is going to double in 7.2 years and you will end up quite wealthy after 20 years.

My mentor, Richard Russell, demonstrated the power of compound interest in his *Dow Theory Letters*. Consider investor A, who opens an investment retirement account (IRA) at age 19. For eight consecutive years he puts $2000 into his IRA each year. At an average growth rate of 10 percent, he will make more money than Investor B, who makes no contributions until age 27 and then contributes $2000 per year every year until she's 65, and earns the same theoretical 10 percent a year. Because of the miracle of compound interest, Investor A, who invested only $16,000 over eight years, ends up with more money than Investor B, who invested $78,000 over 39 consecutive years, but started at a later age. Both invested $2000 per year, both earned the same theoretical 10 percent interest rate. The eight early years of compounding for Investor A were worth more than all of Investor B's additional 31 contributions.

TRADING LIKE A MILLIONAIRE

There are two key elements of what I consider a millionaire's approach to making money. First, millionaires are interested in preserving capital first and foremost. They do not want to lose money. Second, they do not need to trade the markets. They can pick and choose the trades they want, or "cherry-pick." Millionaires don't feel pressured to make money by trading in the markets. Therefore, they tend to invest on the basis of perceived value and excellent risk/reward potential, taking choice trading opportunities in their favor. They will pass on trade after trade, until they find exactly what they want. In other words, they let the market come to them. They are patient and wait until this occurs.

Money must be disciplined, managed, and budgeted—just as time must be scheduled, managed, and budgeted, or else it tends to disappear, as in magic shows. According to Thomas Stanley in *The Millionaire Next Door* (Longstreet, 1996), the truly rich are more interested in seeing their money grow than they are in spending it. This is why the typical American millionaires tend to live in the same town their entire adult life, pay attention to their own small business, maintain a stable personal life, stay married to the same spouse, raise a family in a middle-class neighborhood, and become compulsive savers and investors who are willing to pay top dollar for professional financial advice. Warren Buffett, for example, drives a used car and lives in a modest home. The typical millionaires in this country are always learning and growing and keeping tabs on their money.

They know the value of good advice too. To make money, millionaires are willing to spend money—on investment newsletters, research, and seminars. They realize that their money and assets are always vulnerable: when they earn it, when they spend it, when they invest it, when they get sued, when they are taxed on it, when they live in a high-crime zone, when they are caught in civil unrest or wartime, when the government inflates the currency, and when they die. In other words, our money is always vulnerable to loss, and so we have to keep close tabs on it to keep from losing it.

Other perspectives are useful in understanding money. Wall Street guru Victor Niederhoffer, author of *The Education of a Speculator* (John Wiley & Sons, 1998), has discussed human nature and risk. Here are some of the lessons he has learned in his life:

1. The prey with only one escape route is quickly cornered. In other words, you should always have an alternative plan in case your investment doesn't work out. Seldom does what you have originally hoped for take place in a market.

2. The greatest killings are made during times of panic. You find bargains then that everyone else has sold.

3. Don't invest more than you can afford to lose.

4. Recognize that trends always change.

5. Disaster always lies coiled in safety. People like the comfort of herds when they choose investments. Investing is risky and so investors have to be willing to take risks and act on their own.

MCMASTER'S TEN PRIMARY PRINCIPLES

I formulated ten primary principles for my children and clients for handling their money. Money is like fire: If used within boundaries and carefully monitored, it can be a wonderful servant. Out of control and undisciplined, however, money enslaves and consumes. Here are my ten primary principles:

1. Money should be used primarily to develop and utilize your talents and skills. When applied with hard work and an eye toward service and a long-term view in the marketplace, money will return your initial capital investment many times.

2. Never borrow money for consumer items. You borrow from the future by mortgaging the past to consume in the present. The borrower is slave to the lender. "What really makes the pursuit of convenience and instant gratification [from the use of credit cards] dangerous is that they anesthetize you to the pain

of spending," Stephen M. Pollan and Mark Levine wrote in *Die Broke: A Radical, Four-Part Financial Plan to Restore Your Confidence, Increase Your Net Worth, and Afford You the Lifestyle of Your Dreams* (Harper Business, 1997). "And like any effective painkiller they're both habit forming and constantly require greater doses for you to get the same effect."

The only thing I would consider borrowing for is something that will improve my skills, provide additional education, improve my health, provide a business or solid investment opportunity, or will generate more money.

3. Tithe the first 10 percent of your income. Save the second 10 percent and invest it. Budget the remaining 80 percent. Live by the 80/20 rule. Unless money is watched carefully, unless you keep a close eye on it and budget it, it tends to disappear.

4. Invest your money. The slow but sure way to riches is via the miracle of compound interest. The most important rule of investing is to preserve your capital (money). In other words, money management or risk control has priority over earning more money. A good defense is more important than a good offense when it comes to money. As long as you preserve your capital, you are in the game. It is easy to get into something, like an investment (or a relationship), and it is usually more difficult to get out of it. You may think all it takes to unwind a trade is a phone call to your broker. But making the decision can be the hard part. The decision to take profits or cut losses can be emotional after you have your time, money, and energy at stake. Therefore, thoroughly investigate before you trade. The greater the risk in an investment or trade, the greater the potential reward, but also the greater the potential loss. Consider the potential loss of capital first before considering the potential gain. It is easier to make money than it is to keep it. As previously noted, when you lose half your money, you must make 100 percent on what remains just to get back to breakeven, not considering taxes or inflation. This is not an easy task to accomplish.

5. Live below your means. You will gain both a psychological and a financial buffer for the unexpected contingencies and emergencies in life. Besides, joy comes primarily from above and within, not from material things that stem from the environment.

6. Take care of what you own. Being a good steward and taking good care of your possessions is a form of saving that precludes the need to spend on replacement items. Moreover, fashion, or keeping up with the Joneses, is expensive.

7. Never loan money to a close friend or relative. If you do so, consider it a gift, both mentally and emotionally. Loaning money tends to make enemies.

8. Use OPE (other people's energy) and OPM (other people's money) to increase your wealth rapidly.

I am not a big proponent of debt. One of the root meanings of the word *debt* is death. There is a reason, too, that the French root of the word *mortgage* is death (*mort* = death and *gage* = pledge). Using leverage, margin, and debt, you assume you can accurately predict the future, and so increase your exposure to risk. When you borrow, you mortgage the past to invest in the present on the basis of an uncertain future, with assets and income you can't guarantee you will have.

However, I am very much in favor of using OPE by building a synergistic team of partners, independent contractors, and/or employees, as Napoleon Hill recommends in *Think and Grow Rich* (Ballantine Books, 1996). Life equals time, which equals energy, which equals money. The more lives, time, and energy we synergistically bring to a business activity, the greater the likelihood of a large return.

I also fancy the use of OPM via stock offerings, partners' capital contributions, and limited partnerships as a way to get rich more quickly.

When I started as a freewheeling, hair-on-fire, futures commodity trader and became increasingly successful, I wanted to preserve what I'd made. I didn't want to risk all of it on trades in the market. So I invested in oil well drilling ventures, a llama ranch, cattle ranches, timber, a health food business, and even some good, old-fashioned unleveraged investments in blue chip stocks.

9. Enjoy your money, primarily through increasing the welfare of others, and secondarily, that of yourself. If you want to enjoy your wealth and not have it enslave you, give some of it away.

10. Leave an inheritance, but not at the expense of your own needs here and now. As the authors point out in *Die Broke,* even the expectation of inheritance is inefficient and can be harmful to the giver, the recipient, the entire family, and society. Inheritance can also produce guilt. "The child is put in the position of being hurt by the parent's pursuit of happiness and pleasure. And the parent is forced to choose quality of death over quality of life." The authors say that for inheritance to work, it should not be an entitlement caused by an accident of birth, but should be part of a contract in which the inheritance is earned. They recommend treating "your assets as resources to be used while you're alive rather than treasures to be hoarded for use after you're dead." They even go so far as to say, "The last check you write should be to your undertaker . . . and it should bounce."

To the extent that you do have assets to leave to future generations, I believe that grandchildren are better stewards of money than your own children. The old American saying is "Shirtsleeves to shirtsleeves in three generations." It is also true that grandchildren usually have more in common with the values and interests of grandparents than children have with their parents. For one thing, your children often have a lifetime invested in rebelling against your values. When your grandchildren rebel against their parents, they often find themselves sharing your sentiments and values. The tendency of grandparents to lavish attention and gifts on their grandchildren is also not lost on them.

A FEW MORE RULES

My old friend Harry Browne, who enjoyed years of successful investing, laid down his own rules for financial safety. Here are the ones I find most valuable:*

* Harry Browne, *Special Reports,* Harry Browne Special Reports, Inc., 1997.

1. Your career provides your wealth.
2. Don't assume you can replace your wealth.
3. No trading system will work as well in the future as it did in the past.
4. Recognize the difference between investing and speculating.
5. Don't let anyone make your decisions.
6. Don't ever do anything you don't understand.
7. Keep some assets outside the country in which you live.
8. Beware of tax-avoidance schemes.
9. Don't depend on any one investment or institution for your safety.
10. Create a balanced portfolio for protection.
11. Speculate only with money you can afford to lose.
12. Enjoy yourself with a budget for pleasure.
13. Whenever in doubt about a course of action, err on the side of safety.

As your successful trading increases your pool of money, you should become a successful investor as well. This involves investing in stocks, bonds, real estate, and the like. It's important to get the information and tools you need to be as successful investing as you have been trading. Toward this end, I have long done a complimentary exchange of my bimonthly investment newsletter, *The Reaper,* for the well-known *Dick Davis Digest.* The *Dick Davis Digest* provides analysis of companies and stocks that I don't have time to research personally. For example, I'd never find all the real estate investment trusts (REITs), utilities, bonds, or natural resource stocks they come up with that are worth investing in. Even though I follow the oil market very closely, the *Dick Davis Digest* uncovers oil company stocks I would never otherwise know about. I also learned ways to make money, ways to lose money, and eternal truths regarding good and bad stock investing.

Table 2.3 offers some investment tips that are crucial to the successful handling of money.

The people who make the most money in mutual funds are the owners of the mutual fund companies. Starting your own mutual fund the last few years was the surest way to make

TABLE 2.3 Surefire Ways to Lose and Make Money

Easy Ways to Lose Money	Long-Term Ways to Make Money
• Invest for the short term.	• Invest for the long term.
• Don't diversify.	• Diversify.
• Get emotional about investments you own.	• Be objective about your investments.
• Don't worry about commissions or fees.	• Buy America's best companies and manage your cost of ownership
• Don't worry about the tax consequences.	• Only sell when you need the money or have a sell signal, considering tax consequences.
• Welcome tips from cold-calling brokers.	• Be picky and carefully research and choose your investments.
	• Learn to trust yourself.
• Don't trust yourself.	• Learn from your mistakes.
• Dwell on your past investing mistakes.	• Create your own mini-mutual fund of 5 to 8 of America's best companies or choose carefully the mutual fund companies in which you invest.
• Go ahead and invest in only mutual funds.	

The Staton Institute Advisory, March, 1998, ISBN 800-779-7175.

money. Frankly, though, it's a bit late in the game for that, and not many people have the capital or know-how to pull it off. There are already more mutual funds than there are stocks listed on the New York Stock Exchange. We are covered up with over 7000 mutual funds. When a market is saturated, as the mutual fund market is, there is significantly reduced opportunity for profit for new entrants. A number of mutual funds could go under by the year 2000.

At the very least, don't think of mutual funds as a magic elixir or a sure thing. There is an overabundance of confidence in mutual funds, mostly because of their successful marketing propaganda and the stock bull market. So it pays to be as cautious when selecting a mutual fund as you would be picking a stock. Look for funds with at least a five-year track record, a solid capital base, and money managers who are stable and reputable. Read the prospectus and know what your rights are.

Be willing to allocate your resources among mutual funds; don't consider the diversity within one fund's portfolio to be adequate for your investment portfolio. What percentage of your investment assets are you willing to put in the washed-out Asian stock market right now? Decide how much of your investment portfolio you want to devote to stocks, bonds, foreign currencies, and so on.

The *Dick Davis Digest* presented an investment report by United and Babson about some disastrous eternal truths regarding bad stock investing. They include the following: overreaching for yield; playing hopscotch with investments; acting on tips and information from insiders; being unwilling to take a loss; playing too many speculative and cyclical stocks; buying nothing but low-priced issues; following fashions in stocks; failing to get the facts; and failing to exercise patience. Doing these things are all tried-and-true ways of losing money in stocks.

One of the most successful investors in U.S. history was Bernard Baruch. James Grant, publisher of the highly respected newsletter *Grant's Interest Rate Observer* and author of the biography *Bernard M. Baruch: The Adventures of a Wall Street Legend* (John Wiley & Sons, 1997), listed the aspects of Bernard

Baruch's life that made him successful. These appeared in the well-known newsletter, *Bottom Line:*

1. Act on your convictions—and avoid the crowd.
2. Hold firm opinions, but be open to changing them when another outcome is inevitable.
3. The secret of success is knowing more than everyone else.
4. Be imaginative enough to deduce where the future is brightest.
5. Take risks, but put prudence ahead of profits.

There is a supernatural and a natural aspect to money. Money is at the other end of the spectrum from spirit. I define spirit as living energy with personality, purpose, and power-consciousness. Spirit in time-space is manifested as energy or frequency. When energy and frequency slow down below the speed of light, they set up a standing electromagnetic wave and become matter. When matter has consciousness, it becomes life. Your money is nothing more than a representation of your life, your energy, your time, and your spirit. Money is a reflection of how you spend your time and energy. Money is stored life, stored matter, and stored energy or frequency, all within the aspect of time, and is in the final analysis an aspect of spirit.

As I have endeavored to convey in this chapter, it is important to keep money in perspective—to appreciate what it can and cannot do for you, and to know how to preserve and increase it.

USING MONEY MANAGEMENT TO MANAGE RISK

Numerous successful and sophisticated money management techniques are available today. As we mentioned in Chapter 1, there are three money management rules a trader must set up concerning the allocation of personal financial assets.

Rule 1: Decide how much of your capital you're willing to devote to trading. I recommend keeping $50,000 in your trading account; at the very least, $20,000.

Rule 2: Decide how much you're willing to trade in any particular market sector, such as 20 percent in currencies, 30 percent in stocks, 20 percent in bonds, and 30 percent in commodities.

Rule 3: Compute how much you are willing to risk on any individual trade. A good rule of thumb is to trade no more than 2 to 5 percent of your initial capital on any one trade. If you have $50,000 in trading capital, you would put no more than $2500, or 5 percent, in any individual trade. This means you have to be wrong on 20 consecutive trades to wipe out your capital.

Besides deciding how much money you are willing to trade and how much money you're willing to risk, you also need to ask yourself how much time, energy, and emotion, and how much of your life, you want to put into trading. Will trading pay you enough for it to be worth your while?

Generally, I operate according to the 80/20 rule. About 80 percent of the time I expect to optimize the results I am attempting to achieve. Allow me to explain. Let's say it takes 100 percent of your time, effort, energy, and money to reach the 80 percent success mark in trading. To reach 90 percent may require another 100 percent commitment in time, and 100 percent more money. Where do you come into balance? How do you optimize? We live in a world that has unlimited options and opportunities. Yet we have limited time, limited information, limited energy, and limited money. I have found the 80/20 rule to be effective in bringing balance to my life. I want to do whatever I do competently, effectively, and efficiently. But I don't have to be the best or perfect. Being the best or perfect draws down too much of me in one area and causes me to be out of balance in other important areas of my life. My pursuit instead is for excellence. In search of balance, you must decide how much of your life you're willing to commit to trading.

If money management is a weakness in your personal or professional life, you may want to spend more of your trading time on this area to reach optimization. But even if it is an area in which you are relatively stable, I would consider giving money management primary emphasis. Twenty percent of your trades make 80 percent of your money, and 20 percent of your trades may lead to 80 percent of your losses of financial capital. The other 60 percent of the time you will be "chopping around" with breakevens, small wins, or small losses. Therefore, money management is a must for financial survival.

The more sophisticated the techniques that people attempt to master in trading and money management, the less frequently they will use those techniques. If you have to put too much time, energy, money, or life into any particular thing and its payoff is not commensurate, you tend to reduce your commitment to it. Accordingly, it loses its marginal utility.

be wrong about being bullish and you will exit the trade. In other words, you will leave a protective stop loss at $5.40. Since each cent in a silver futures contract is worth $50, a 10-cent drop in silver prices from your $5.50 entry point to your $5.40 protective stop loss means that you will be risking $500 ($50 × 10) per contract on the silver trade. Since you have decided to risk $2500 on each trade, you know in this silver trade that you can purchase five contracts of silver ($2500 ÷ $500 = 5 contracts). You have effectively backed into the number of contracts you are going to trade. The point is, you want all your trades to have equal risk, regardless of what you're trading. This approach prevents you from wiping out nice wins in orange juice, lean hogs, or gold through one loss in, say, S&P futures.

DO YOUR HOMEWORK THE NIGHT BEFORE YOU TRADE

To preserve psychological capital, I prefer to do my homework (plan my trades) for the markets the night before so my left-brain activity is completed. Then I can sleep on the trades I've planned and let my subconscious and right brain contemplate what I've already worked out in my left brain. If the prospective trade feels good when I wake up in the morning, and the markets are starting to track in harmony with the way I had anticipated the night before, I don't have the drawdown of psychological capital when I'm trading. My balanced-risk approach to trading, in terms of money management, which I describe in greater detail in Chapter 6, makes it easy for me to take the trade; it reduces the fear, the greed, and the uncertainty that can cause traders to stumble and burn up their psychological and financial capital. Planning ahead allows your right-brain intuition to identify signals or other important details that your left-brain analysis may have missed.

Again, a key to preserving psychological capital is that *you* determine risk, not the market. You balance risk among the various futures contracts, which you can compute with relative certainty. There is no anxiety from second-guessing or imbalance in trading.

PYRAMID EQUITY, NOT CONTRACTS

Many traders like to pyramid a trading position—increasing their position in the stock or futures markets. There are two ways to do so. The first method, standard pyramiding of shares or contracts, involves leveraging open profits as they accrue on paper (but before the contract expires)—a sure way to violate your money management system by allowing the market to determine your exposure to profit and loss. For example, if you buy 500 shares of IBM and the price of IBM stock goes up, as it goes up you may buy another 300 shares. Then if IBM moves higher, you may buy another 200 shares. As IBM continues to move up, you may buy yet another 100 shares. This way you build a pyramid on the basis of your profits as they accrue in the midst of a trade. The problem with pyramiding shares or contracts is that if the market has already moved in your favor, the odds are greater that the market will then move against you—at the same time that you are betting on the market continuing its current trend. A small correction can wipe out your hard-earned profits when you pyramid.

The second approach, pyramiding your equity instead of contracts, allows you to be more aggressive without violating your money management system and without increasing market risk. Using our previous example, say you risk $2500 in a trade and you make $5000 net profit in that initial trade. You now have a choice: You can put your initial $2500 back into its original number 1 slot and bank the $5000 profit, or you can use your $5000 profit to pyramid your equity on your next several trades. You can, for example, increase the amount you trade in the next five trades by $1000 for a total risk per trade of $3500 over the next five trades. If you want to be more aggressive, you can increase the amount of risk in the next two trades by $2500, risking $5000 in each of the next two trades. Either way you're risking your $5000 profit by pyramiding equity. In 1998, when there was deflation in commodities and futures markets, you may have felt confident about being aggressive on the short side, and may have wanted to risk $5000 on each of the next two trades—$2500 of your initial capital plus half the net profit from your first trade ($2500).

Then, if trade number 2 pays off big and gives you, say, a 3-to-1 return, you have done quite well, with a net profit of $15, 000 from that trade with $5000 risk. If you happen to lose, all you've lost of your initial capital is $2500 out of the number 2 slot, and your pyramiding equity ($2500) has not paid off. Still, you are in control of risk and that preserves your financial and psychological capital. This is a great deal different from trying to pyramid (buy more at higher prices) the stock market, the gold market, or the bond or soybean market during a vertical ascent and then getting caught in a correction that takes a big swipe out of your capital. Pyramiding equity as a way of money management rather than pyramiding the number of contracts or shares traded is a better way to go.

As you can see, there are several differences between pyramiding contracts or shares and pyramiding equity. When you pyramid contracts or shares, you are increasing your exposure in a particular trade before the trade has ended. When you pyramid equity, you use actual profit from a completed trade to increase dollars at risk in your next trade. All you can lose is your initial 5 percent of your trading capital and your partial profits from the first trade.

The upside potential is greater with pyramiding. Back in 1994 one of my clients made $40 million on $4 million in coffee futures in less than six months. He was pyramiding both equity and contracts! But he was experienced enough and had enough money to trade big bucks he could afford to lose. He could manage the risk. I am more conservative. I prefer to reduce the variability of unknown factors, the trade-off being a lower return.

CHART YOUR EQUITY

Another useful concept in money management is charting your own equity (see Figure 3.2). First, you chart where your account is. For starters, each day, as you close out your trades, you track

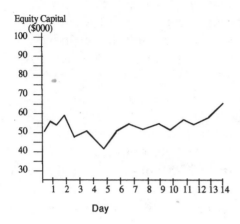

FIGURE 3.2.   Chart of Daily Equity

how much you have added or subtracted from your trading capital. Another approach is to have your broker send you a computer run of your account value, including open and closed trades as well as your margin capital and whatever you're holding in T-bills, at the start of each trading day. You then chart that amount.

Use your equity chart to determine (by way of your own technical analysis) whether you are in a personal bull or bear market. This gives you a very good grasp of who and what you are, and how you're trading. It will minimize what I call the King Kong effect, of thinking you can conquer the market when you're winning. Just about the time you feel this way, you should be prepared to take some losses. Charting your equity provides a useful psychological check on your pride. For instance, when you have a huge equity run-up, you may feel euphoric, or cocky, or complacent about the market. A look at your equity will help you become more cautious instead of complacent or excessively bullish, which might tempt you to ignore your position or get aggressive and add to your position.

On the other hand, if you experience a number of losing or breakeven trades, your emotions might influence you to start to pick and choose your trades more capriciously instead of sticking to your trading system. A peek at your equity chart may indicate that you are looking at the bottom of the market. You will see this is not the time to become risk-averse. Often the very next trade is the one that will make you financially well-off overnight. If you have been charting your equity and you see that you have an oversold buy signal, it's time to stick with your trading program.

Your equity will set up technical chart patterns, and overbought/oversold situations, just as the market does. If you've had a run-up in profits and it's followed by losses that bring you back to consolidation—say, a one-third correction of your increase in equity—you are still in an overall up trend. That's the place to realize your equity has bottomed out. You are due for some more wins. If you hadn't charted your equity, you would not have seen that. Or, when you see a setup in your equity as you would see it in a market by way of a technical oversold buy signal, that also may be a time to consider pyramiding equity. By charting your equity, you have a more objective view of who you are, how you're trading, and when you might consider trading more or less. This will increase your trading discipline.

CUT YOUR LOSSES SHORT

Another standard money management technique is cutting losses short. I cannot emphasize this point enough. Nothing burns up psychological capital and financial capital like letting losses run. Why? We all have limited time, limited information, limited energy, limited knowledge, and limited money. We live in an environment of uncertainty that is becoming increasingly chaotic. If we let our losses run, particularly when we're operating against our trading plan, we're going to burn up our psychological capital as well as our financial capital. Then we'll be out of the game.

> Letting losses ride will force you to focus on problems instead of opportunities.

Failure to cut a loss short, letting a losing trade run against you, letting your position move against you by moving your protective stop loss lower or pulling out of the market altogether, will render your money management plan null and void. You will be risking a higher percentage than allowed on a particular trade. Sticking to your money management system prevents your emotions from playing tricks on you. A solid money management system lets you see what you're doing and helps you analyze more objectively how you're positioned in the market. Good money management is a check on the ruinous practice of letting losses run. When you don't cut losses short and let profits ride, you'll see it quickly in your equity chart line.

Riding losses will consume your mental and emotional energy and draw down on your ability to focus on trading opportunities available elsewhere in the market day to day. Let's say that the market declines, you're long, and you've lost $2500 in S&P futures, but you believe the market will go back up. If you decide not to get out and override your stop loss, your loss the next morning might be $3200. If you continue to let the loss ride, the next day your loss might be $4100. The more the loss builds, the more likely you are to ignore other trading opportunities. The loss becomes the focus of all your mental and emotional efforts—a real drawdown financially and psychologically. You are focusing on problems instead of opportunities. This is a road to ruin.

One of the mistakes many businesses make is to focus on areas where they're losing money or where they have the greatest problems rather than assigning their best personnel to focus on money-making opportunities. What we are talking about here is as true in the markets as it is in business. When you see that the same principle applies consistently across various areas of life, you know you are dealing with a fundamental truth. I call it the harmonics of reality.

MANAGE BY EXCEPTION

Another business management principle that applies to market money management is management by exception. MBE simply says that if things are okay, leave them alone. If it ain't broke, don't fix it. Avoid the temptation to tinker too much, to do too much busywork in search of that elusive, mythical Holy Grail of trading.

Application: If you have profits, let them run. Leave them alone. The "exception" in management by exception is a momentum trade, a setup that has brought you into the market promising an initial burst in your favor, and that's all you can count on. If it doesn't happen, get out! Say you're trading two contracts in this situation. You might also consider taking down your first $1000 profit in the first contract or an initial price burst, then let the second contract ride with the protective stop loss moved up closer to breakeven. Experience has taught me that any time you get a per contract profit above $1000 in futures trading, if you can take part of that profit down by selling a profitable contract, the odds are you'll be better able to let the profits ride on the remaining contract, or exit if MBE kicks in. This approach helps you preserve psychological capital too.

Not that many futures traders end up taking more than a $1000 contract profit out of the futures market. So, to approach that 80 percent optimization, which is equal to a $1000 profit per contract, you might consider banking half the position, taking partial profits on one of the two contracts. This is why I love trading multiple contracts. You want to have a chance to catch the big move, to get beyond 80 percent into the top 20 percent. At the same time, if you can take partial profits in a market, it will help sustain your account and minimize the drawdown if the market turns against you. Preservation of capital is vital. Management by exception says if you have a good system, just execute your plan. If it's running smoothly, just leave it alone, and let profits ride.

KEEP TRACK OF YOUR TRADES WITH A DIARY

Find a few quiet minutes at the end of your trading day, or first thing in the morning, while market details are still fresh in your mind, to chart your number of winners and your number of los-

Trading and money management are easy to learn, but hard to execute.

ers so you can see the results of your own trading and money management techniques—exactly what you're doing month in and month out, year in and year out, in the markets. Every conversation you have with yourself, every insight and thought about your trades, every comment your broker has about your trades, and every mistake you have made are all important elements of your written commentary. Make note of what went on in your mind during trading hours.

I'm old-fashioned; I like to handwrite my diary, just as some people still like to chart the market by hand. There is something about writing a journal manually that gives me a better feel for everything. It helps me bring more insight to the market and it feels more personal. It also forces me to be more honest. Unlike typing on a computer, when you handwrite a diary, you can't just define and delete an entry. You are less likely to edit your thoughts. However, if you are more likely to make regular entries on a computer, that's fine. Do what feels right for you.

Besides making regular entries, you should take the time to review your diary regularly. The whole point is to look back at your diary to gain a perspective on your trading. I usually take one of my old diaries on an airplane when I'm traveling. I have a couple of dozen books now, one for each year I've been trading. I am often amused about some of the things I used to think, feel, and do in the markets. It may be painful to confront how amateurish I have been, but it's also emotionally satisfying to see how much I've grown, how far I've come. It's also important to remember key principles I may have forgotten that I want to reintegrate into my trading. I find it extremely helpful and enlightening to pull out old charts during different periods of my trading, so as I review my diaries, I can see what I was thinking during different market movements.

Capturing all this information will enable you to step back and see your trading patterns, productive and nonproductive.

You will be able to recognize whether you have a bull (going long) or a bear (going short) bias in trade selection. Maybe you want to correct it, maybe you don't. At least you will know who you are, thereby helping preserve not only financial capital but also psychological capital. You are going to school on yourself. The more you know about yourself and the way you approach the markets, the better your trading can be over the long term. Trading and money management are easy to learn, but hard to execute. The more connected you are, the more parts of your brain you're bringing to what you do, and the more focused and effective you will be.

Reviewing your diary on a regular basis will help you pick up points you may have forgotten—positive and negative—that will improve your trading. The more you understand your history, the more you will understand the future and be grounded in the present. As with helping your children do their homework, you pick up items from your diary that you'd forgotten. Speaking of children, your diaries can serve as a legacy for them and your grandchildren. After all, the more people know about their family history, the more grounded they will be as they meet their life challenges.

This perspective flies in the face of the American short-term attitude: "Ignorance is bliss." I prefer an old Lebanese proverb: "Truth kills those who hide from it." Ultimately, you want to have a long-term view if you're going to survive and prosper. Keeping track of your trading moves, thoughts, and feelings will give you a higher sense of accountability. It will also increase your discipline in sticking to your trading and money management systems.

The market is an environment of uncertainty and risk. The points in this chapter will help you use sound money management to increase certainty and minimize risk as much as you possibly can in your own approach to the marketplace.

THE BUSINESS OF THE TRADE

One of the key mistakes that traders make is not treating their trading of the markets as a business. Entrepreneurs who fail often can trace their demise to having ignored basic small-business principles. Traders need a similar set of guidelines to follow to ensure that they trade in a businesslike manner.

I have formulated eight principles of a good business, listed in Table 4.1, which apply equally to entrepreneurs starting a small business and to traders. Now, let's apply these principles to *The Art of the Trade*.

MAKE MONEY

The purpose of trading is to make money. Unless you have a trading methodology that can make money in some consistent manner, there's no reason to be involved in *The Art of the Trade*. You are not in the markets for fun, for excitement, for challenge, for stimulation, or to punish yourself. You are in the markets to make money.

An important criterion for making money is to keep costs low. You don't necessarily need a fancy office with expensive furnishings, or a large number of employees. You do not need to update your computer systems or software constantly, or invest

TABLE 4.1 McMaster's Eight M's of a Good Business

1) It has to make Money.
2) It has to be Meaningful.
3) It has to have good Men behind it.
4) It has to have enough Money.
5) It has to have good Management.
6) It has to be a Moral business.
7) It has to have a Market and be Marketable.
8) It has to have a Marketing plan.

huge amounts in research and development. Focus on substance, not style, not flash. The best investment you can make is in your own knowledge and skills, and the equipment necessary to trade profitably. Spend the money on the tools you need to help you accomplish your trade, to apply your system profitably, or to increase your skill level. But don't overinvest for a marginal return.

Just as a mature focus on important responsibilities and mental toughness are critical to a successful small business, so they are vital to your success as a trader. It is important for you to focus on what makes you money, what pays off. Do what's important. Do not participate in activities that are nonproductive or marginal. You also don't need to overspend for advice on how to trade successfully. You might subscribe to half a dozen market newsletters, but not 30 of them. You need to discover your niche too, what works for you, and then get on with the business of trading.

I have found that the three best ways to invest your money and your time are:

- In your own skills
- In your own business

- In your own investments close to home that you personally handle

Your ability to make money with any given trading system depends on your personal and professional state of mind. Someone who's struggling in life to make ends meet and is being supported by a spouse or other family members, who is moving from job to job, isn't going to have the character or work habits necessary to be a successful trader. You must have it together in your personal and professional life before you can come to the markets and hope to trade successfully on a consistent basis. Otherwise, you may have too much at stake emotionally on every trade, and you will be unlikely to stick to your trading and money management systems. Your faulty work habits and unprofessional behavior will do you in trading the markets. Success in your personal and professional life does not guarantee success in the markets; however, it is a necessary ingredient of successful trading.

FIND A MEANINGFUL SYSTEM

Your trading system (usually technical) has to be meaningful and have a proven track record. It should not be one of those fly-by-night schemes that are too often pandered to market traders as a way to become a millionaire overnight. There are many opportunists in the advertising community willing to sell the latest get-rich-quick system to some gullible trader. A comprehensive approach to trading the market will have its strengths and its weaknesses, but the acid test is that it must be consistently profitable over time.

A reputable trading system should go back and trade past markets theoretically, to see how a particular trading method would have worked. You can purchase trading software programs that have been tested on historical market data, that traders have used and endorsed, that have been validated. But be careful; some software trading programs out there have not really tested the markets fully, have "doctored" their results, or have not traded during real time. Find reviews in publications such as *Technical Analysis of Stocks and Commodities, Futures* magazine, and *Commodity Trader's Consumer Report.* A good number of books, such as Jack D. Schwager's *Market Wizards: Interviews with Top Traders* (Harper Business, 1993) and *The New Market Wizards: Conversations with America's Top Traders* (Harper Business, 1994), can also help you find a system that works for you. One of the best sources on reliable technical systems is John Hill of Futures Truth Company (815 Hillside Road, Hendersonville, NC 28739).

As I discuss in Chapter 5, no proven system, regardless of its track record, is inherently good or bad. A system's ability to help you trade successfully and make money depends on the degree to which it fits your personality, which in turn determines your ability to stick with the system during tough market times.

FIND GOOD PEOPLE

A good business has to have good people behind it to operate successfully. As described in Chapter 1, you need to look for a track record of success and integrity. Whether you are just starting out on your own or you are a seasoned, professional trader with a staff of researchers who help you follow the markets you trade, surround yourself with people you trust, people who are also professionally competent.

Much of this trading business involves buying and selling over the phone with a broker, where your word is your bond. The broker's word and your word are effectively a contract. Dealing in unethical or immoral businesses can result in huge losses financially and/or psychologically. You cannot afford to lose your financial or psychological capital. Doing a background check, as well as looking at the historical track record of the brokers with whom you are doing business, is a must. Brokerage firms and advisory services come and go. It is wise to trade with ones that are established, even if they cost a little more. Ask the brokerage firm, investment firm, or advisory service for personal, up-to-date references. You are hiring them to work for you. You want to make sure that they have a record of being accountable and that they deliver accurate, honest, and professional services.

INVEST MONEY IN YOUR TRADING BUSINESS

A good business, particularly a new business, needs to have plenty of money. It needs to be well capitalized, with a cushion at least 20 percent above what you compute to be necessary. Murphy's Law states that if something can go wrong, it will. You need a cushion of financial capital, of financial staying power, for those unanticipated costs in any business, including your trading business.

Studies show that among businesses that failed, 93 percent were undercapitalized. Year after year, statistics indicate this is the main reason small traders fail too. They have underestimated the need for capital in their account. They start out without enough money. They are therefore unable to diversify over enough markets and trades to spread out their risks. This diminishes the staying power necessary to withstand drawdowns (losses). The sad fact of trading is that a series of sustained losses is part of any trader's history. That's just part of the trading life. Also, insufficient capital means you will be unable to spread your trading risk over a number of markets to diversify successfully.

The rock-bottom capital you should devote to your trading is $20,000. This is money you should consider to be risk capital, money you can afford to lose without blinking an eye. It should not be from your individual retirement account (IRA) or your children's college fund. In addition, you need to have cash on hand to take care of your business and personal expenses while you're trading, particularly if you're trading exclusively for a living (not a good idea). Not having this pool of capital available puts too much stress on you, forcing you to look desperately for profitable trades. The inevitable result is just the opposite: poor choices and usually losses. The pressure to trade this way is just too intense.

PRACTICE SOUND MANAGEMENT

A good business must be managed correctly. Trading is a business. It requires attention to detail, accounting, money management, trade selection, and a broad range of managerial activities that are used in any successful business. This is what ensures long-term success for the trader. Just as a winning professional football team requires a solid support system of competent management, such as coaches, trainers, and administrators, so a successful trader needs the business foundation to trade profitably long term.

The KISS principle applies here. There is so much for a trader to do, just as there is so much to do in a small business. But there is only so much we can do. We have limited time. Schedule and prioritize responsibilities. It is helpful to do the most important things in the trading business rather than the urgent things.

Important Activities to Pursue. Review your trading system daily to ascertain if it has triggered or is about to trigger buy or sell signals. Check to make sure your previous trade executions were correct, including the futures contract month, number of contracts, number of shares, and price. Ensure that your protective stop losses are placed correctly in the market and that the original margin capital in your account is placed in Treasury bills or a money market fund to earn interest while you are in or out of trades. Update your daily log of activities, thoughts, and insights, and your equity chart. Review your trading system for possible improvements and check out indicators you may want to add to increase the system's accuracy.

Distractions to Avoid. Dodge the black hole of always trying to overly refine or improve your trading system. In terms of fundamental trading, refrain from excessive reading and analysis in the false hope you can get a comprehensive understanding of all the factors that influence a particular market. No amount of reading or analysis will enable you to predict the markets with total accuracy.

We all have daily distractions in life that make it easy to lose perspective on what is important versus what is urgent: a child's baseball game, a friend to visit in the hospital, overtime on the job, a crisis with a family member. Just as you won't engage in physical exercise regularly unless you schedule and make time for it, so you must display a similar discipline with trading, even when other priorities are screaming at you. Trading doesn't scream at you. It will let you fill up your life with endless other activities, many of which are worthy, and trading will die. Professional trading requires self-imposed attention and the discipline to approach it consistently.

Especially when you experience a series of losses, which are painful, it's easy to succumb to all these other dutiful and/or fun priorities that can help you feel good about yourself and give you a reason to escape the responsibilities of trading. Many people have to do good to feel good. If they aren't doing well at a particular activity, they will tend to move to some other activity that they can do well, which allows them to feel good about themselves. Other people need to feel good to do good. If they don't feel good about their trading, they will tend to do something else to help them feel good so their trading will improve.

Depending on the technical trading system you use, you don't need to follow the markets all day. (One notable exception is if you are a day trader, who trades in and out of the markets constantly.) I like to do my analysis the night before, then enter my orders the next morning. Once your system is up and running—which can be time-consuming at first—it should not require too much time to implement.

One of the most important management tactics is your protective stop loss. Without one, you could be wrong a number of times in a row and have large drawdowns. Protective stop losses are a market brake on the distractions of life.

LIFE

No one ever said
Life was a piece of cake
It comes all mixed up
Full of its own shake and bake.

We try to shape our lives
To fit a plan, pattern, or mold
But life's twists and turns
Weave a story all their own.

We'd love to figure life out
Remove all risk and insecurities
But finding joy in each new day
Is a mark of growing maturity.

Life is often difficult
Occasionally is easy
It rewards the strong of heart
It takes its toll on the queasy.

So we might as well relax
Flow with the good and the bad
Rejoice in sunshine and in shadow
Embrace the happy with the sad.

APPLY SOLID MORALS

The trading business needs to be moral. Besides choosing to deal with people you trust, you must take the moral high ground yourself. Trading presents many challenges to your moral strength. Particularly when a trader faces a loss, it can be tempting to blame the broker, claiming the broker did not execute the order properly. That's why so many brokerage firms, which have had so much trouble with traders disputing their orders or violating verbal agreements, have resorted to recording conversations with their clients and repeating orders back to them for the record.

It is actually in your own self-interest not to lie to your broker about such things. If you lie to your broker, you are lying to yourself—about how well you're doing, who's fault it is when a trade goes sour. You will look for excuses instead of learning from your mistakes, and will short-circuit your ability to make profitable trades in the future.

You must look honestly at what the market is doing, how well the trading system is working, and your own strengths and weaknesses. It takes tremendous discipline and self-knowledge to trade successfully. Taking the moral high ground enhances your ability to see and approach the markets objectively and thus profitably.

STICK WITH SOUND MARKETS THAT YOU KNOW WELL

Just as entrepreneurs should never jump into a business they do not understand, it is best for traders to avoid exotic trades, and trades they do not understand. Look to trade in markets that have considerable liquidity and are well established. Trade in markets where you have some working understanding of the fundamentals that affect price. This will help you avoid painful losses. Unnecessary surprises often occur in exotic, little-traded, and sparsely followed markets where you are probing in the dark.

However, exotic is largely subjective. To someone inexperienced in Asian markets, any investment there may seem exotic, even one that is well established, with considerable liquidity. Steer clear of trades you find confusing; avoid spreading or arbitrage strategies that are complicated to you.

DEVELOP A MARKETING AND BUSINESS PLAN

You will need a marketing plan to help you decide how to allocate your trading money in line with your trading approach to a particular market. It has to be well thought out, both strategically and tactically.

At least three-fourths of small businesses that have failed had a weak business plan. A business plan includes a clear statement of the owner's objectives and timetable and a thorough analysis of the business, what kinds of systems it needs to oper-

> Trades are often like children. If they are monitored and cared for, they do well. If they are ignored and neglected, they tend to become rebellious, cause trouble, and result in losses.

ate, and what kinds of procedures are required. The approach is no different in the trading markets. The elements of a trader's business plan include how much you will spend on research and development, systems, office equipment, and furnishings, as well as your time allocation and what returns you expect your trading to yield. Compute this on an hourly basis. If you're a $200-per-hour attorney and you project (or experience) that you will make (or have made) $100 an hour from trading over the months, maybe you should decide it makes more economic sense to spend more time at your job—unless your purpose is to have fun in the markets and learn and grow. That's okay, but just make sure your projections don't conflict with the objectives you include in your business plan. Your business plan should also outline your personal growth: how much time you will give yourself on the learning curve to meet your objectives.

Small business owners tend to overestimate sales and underestimate costs. Similarly, traders tend to overestimate profits and underestimate potential losses. This sets the groundwork for failure. Your business plan will help you make more realistic projections and outline what it will take to become successful.

Not many entrepreneurs would attempt to run a business about which they knew nothing. They may hire a consultant or manager who is proven competent in that particular business and do plenty of research before jumping in. Yet for some reason, perhaps because people use money all the time in life, aspiring traders assume that trading does not require the same professional approach as launching a business.

It should now be obvious how trading has to meet the requirements of a good business if it is to be successful. You will be continually learning and growing, investing in your own skills to improve your trading, so you become better at your "trade," or *The Art of the Trade*. Trading is a business that you must run and manage if it is to do well financially. Trades are often like children. If they are monitored and cared for, they do well. If they are ignored and neglected, they tend to become rebellious, cause trouble, and result in losses.

AVOID COMMON BUSINESS MISTAKES

Now let's compare the worst mistakes that small business owners make with the worst mistakes new traders make. You will find that they are very similar.

Lack of Objective Advice.   Poor advice causes traders to become too subjective. They tend to rush to a market too quickly, before they've done their homework. New traders are often tempted to trade on hot tips. I've never known a successful trader who traded on tips from others as the basis for a trading approach. When you get a hot tip on a stock or commodity, first check it out before you invest or trade. Don't believe everything you hear. Many new traders also tend to be too subjective about the advice that they use in making decisions. You need to have good objective filters—research about proven trading systems and how to pull together a successful trading business—in order to help you formulate your business plan and trading approach to the markets. You need a realistic strategy. Avoid rushing into trades in the hopes of making fast profits. Do not use a new system to trade the market before you have had a chance to test it, adjust to it, and become comfortable with it.

The greatest bargain available is the low cost of good advice. Good advice helps you pull together all the information that's out there to make solid decisions. Unfortunately, over the past couple of decades, when I have been called upon as a consultant to help traders, it is often after they are already in trouble and need help getting out of it. I find it is important to communicate how they got themselves into their predicament in the first place, so they can better recover and prevent it from happening again. One recurring theme I see among traders in trouble is that their complex personal and professional life requires so much mental and emotional focus and drawdown of psychologi-

It doesn't matter if the glass is half empty or half full, it matters which way the trend is moving. Once you know the trend, you can make money.

cal capital that they simply don't have the reserves or the reflective quiet time they need to trade successfully.

Big Egos That Inhibit Doing Business Successfully.   Too many traders find that their egos, their desire to be correct rather than to make money, get in the way of trading successfully. Ego involvement leads to inflexibility in trading and to problems such as failure to cut losses short. Humility and flexibility are two of the most important characteristics a small business owner and a trader can have. Humility and flexibility allow you to move quickly, to be responsive to the market.

Being in Too Many Businesses at Once.   Traders will find themselves stretched too thin if they're involved in too many trades simultaneously. Each trade requires their full attention in order to maximize profits or minimize losses. There is no substitute for focused attention on a business or trade.

Believing All the Good News from the Media.   Basing your feel for the market on the incessant flow of good news from the investment and financial media is a sure way to go with the crowd and move with the herd as it runs over a cliff. You must be realistic in the trading business—not necessarily optimistic or pessimistic. Remember, money can be made on both the long side and the short side. In other words, it doesn't matter if the glass is half empty or half full; it matters which way the trend is moving. Once you know the trend, you can make money.

ARISTOTLE'S TRADING TIPS

Throughout the centuries, the procedures necessary to be successful in business have remained remarkably constant. After all, human nature, which dictates business approaches, has not changed. For example, the Greek philosopher Aristotle's views on business and trading apply today just as much as ancient times.

A Theory Is Nice, but Experience Is What Count
true in both business and trading. What works is what counts and only experience tells you what works. A good entrepreneur or good trader will implement and apply techniques that have been proven, that have a vast realm of experience behind them.

Precision in Thought Is Very Important. In trading, attention to detail can make a huge difference in rate of return. There is no substitute for the professionalism of precision. You can be right about the direction of a market long term, but if your entry is poorly timed, you can lose money. You could fine-tune your market entry and exit points by using 5-minute bar charts (the highest, lowest, and latest prices traded in the last five minutes) and other technical indicators. Fine-tuned entry and exit procedures can help you pick up a few points here and there, and over a year this will increase your annual percentage returns significantly.

For example, on a weekly or daily bar chart, the entry point into a long position in silver might be $5.55. But by doing microanalysis of the 5-minute and 15-minute bar charts, you might be able to fine-tune your trigger point for entry to $5.53. Because each cent of a silver futures contract is worth $50, you can therefore pick up another $100 per contract on market entry by being precise.

Unity of Purpose Must Be Achieved to Realize Success.
Success is impossible long term without character and virtue. Further, it is important to do the right thing at the right time. Character and virtue are the glue that hold together thought, emotion, and behavior in a unified, harmonious way.

PETER DRUCKER'S FIVE DEADLY BUSINESS SINS

World famous management consultant Peter Drucker, author of *The Executive in Action: Managing for Results, Innovation, and Entrepreneurship—The Effective Executive* (Harper Business, 1996), formulated five deadly business sins, which have direct application to the success or failure of a trader.

The Worship of High Profit Margin and Premium Pricing. Premium pricing creates a market for competitors and invites them to steal your market share. Your huge profit margin leaves room for them to offer the same product or service for less money. When desktop computers and faxes first came out, for example, original manufacturers' huge profit margins gave competitors room to steal market share by taking a smaller profit margin. The competitors were able to lock up the market and discourage newer competitors from entering the fray. In similar fashion, a trader needs to think twice about buying stock in a company that has this short-term advantage reflected in earnings. These earnings could disappear through price-cutting competition in the not too distant future.

Mispricing a New Product by Charging What the Market Will Bear. Mispricing creates a risk-free opportunity for a competitor. It is akin to a trader looking to squeeze the last cent of profit out of a trade, rather than taking a reasonable profit. It's like a manufacturer charging $2000 for fax machines when they were new to the market. It's also like looking to sell gold at $900 an ounce in 1980, rather than $735. Price never got there. Greed that the gold price would go higher (to $1000), and traders' fear that they would miss the move, led to their not taking a healthy profit or buying an overpriced asset. The U.S. stock market in July 1998 is another example.

Markets always come back to the equilibrium of value. You should be very careful before you buy in an overvalued market or sell in an undervalued market. History is working against you. Greed and fear are the worst enemies of a trader. There's an old saying in the market, "Bulls make money and bears make money, but pigs get slaughtered." In other words, being greedy is a certain trap door to losses and failures for a trader.

Bulls make money and bears make money, but pigs get slaughtered.

Cost-driven Pricing.   The only thing that works is price-driven costing. Consider how many people can afford to purchase a Rolls Royce. Not many. A Rolls costs a great deal to build and is priced accordingly. A better way to approach a market is to figure out what people are willing and able to pay for a product, and then back into how to design it and build it to meet that market.

Successful traders are just as responsive to the market. They wait and let the market tell them what opportunities exist. Then they respond accordingly. They don't force their thinking or position on the market. Such will only result in losses. Successful traders use signals, not wild hunches; they listen to the market and take whatever opportunities for profits it provides them. For instance, many traders have a bullish bias when it comes to gold and so always look to go long. They see in the gold market bullish evidence that is not there, as an excuse to buy gold, even when the market has told them not to buy through price action, fundamentals, or lack of technically triggered buy signals.

Slaughtering Tomorrow's Opportunity on the Altar of Yesterday.   Living in the past is fatal. Remember IBM preventing its PC people from selling to its potential mainframe customers? As a result, other PC manufacturers did so, and took away a market and clients that were already sitting in IBM's lap.

The past is gone, it's history. It's behind you. There is nothing you can do except learn from your mistakes and your successes, as you record new insights and review old ones in the daily journal that I recommend you keep. Agonizing over yesterday's losses and mistakes—or focusing excessively upon a losing position—comes at the expense of finding new trading opportunities that exist in the market today and that are upcoming tomorrow. When traders focus on the past, they are unconscious in the present. But we live only in the present. We can take action only in the present. We can only trade in the present.

Traders do tend to get stuck. One trader I know made tremendous profits in Coca-Cola because he'd been a blue-chip stock trader all his life, but he missed a wonderful opportunity to buy Microsoft in the 1990s. He was locked into perceptions that had worked quite well for him historically. He did not allow for growth, or for changes that were opening up in the future. Another trader who traded U.S. stocks exclusively missed incredible opportunities to trade profitably over the last couple of years in European stock markets, which soared in anticipation of the introduction of the euro currency, and had far greater returns than U.S. stock markets experienced.

You are alive only in the present, in the now. So today is, in every sense of the word, a *present*. Holding onto the baggage of the past, the mistakes of yesterday, is nonproductive. It robs you of your energy and mental and emotional focus on new opportunities. You must see what opportunities exist now and take advantage of them. This is the only opportunity you really have to profit. Yes, you need to learn from your mistakes, but don't dwell on them. Use them as positive learning experiences; as a springboard to becoming a better trader.

Feeding Problems and Starving Opportunities.   Usually a company's best performers are assigned to problems—to old business. As a result, the company misses the profit opportunities in front of it. Feeding problems can kill a successful trader too. Only opportunities can result in growth and profits. This is where a trader should be focusing, on emerging trading opportunities. Protective stop losses will take care of problematic (losing) trades.

Cut your losses short, eliminate your problems as quickly as possible, and let your profits ride. Focus your time, energy, and money on making money—on new trading opportunities. If you handle your money management and protective stop placement correctly, your profits and losses will take care of themselves. You will be wrong at times. So what? Being wrong is part of life. We all err. If you've done your job correctly, either you will take your loss in keeping with your plan or the situation will turn around into a profit. There's no reason to focus on it once you've initiated the trade. Your focus needs to be on opportunities, upcoming trades that could very well profit you and increase the equity in your trading account. There are no perfect trades. Waiting for the perfect trade is much like a surfer paddling offshore on a surfboard to wait all day long for the perfect wave, as opposed to catching many good ones that will give enjoyable rides. Waiting is exhausting, and you are likely to have very little to show for the effort.

THE METHODOLOGY OF THE TRADE

A trading system is effective only to the extent that the trader actually uses it. There are many pitfalls that cause traders to get sidetracked. First, to get the most out of a trading system, you must select the right type of system for you—one that matches your personality type. Second, a trading system isn't something you should take out of a box and use as is; you must customize it by selecting a mix of indicators that will provide you with left-brain analytical data and enhance your right-brain intuitive sense of the markets. Third, you need to select a mix of indicators that will give you the best feel for the markets and help you follow faithfully the trading system you have chosen. Fourth, you must create an emotional environment that will enable you to continually replenish your psychological capital.

FIND THE BEST TRADING STYLE FOR YOUR PERSONALITY

A trading system with a great track record may work wonders for your sister-in-law or your best friend. Even if you carefully and painstakingly implement every nuance of the same trading system, you may find that it bombs for you, or you're continually tense implementing it. There simply is no one perfect trading system for everyone. One of the key factors that can make or

CHAPTER FIVE

TABLE 5.1 What Is the Best Trading Strategy for Your Personality?

Personality Traits	Most Effective Trading System
• Conservative, risk averse, middle-of-the-road type	• Swing trading, focusing on short-term break-out moves, or spring-board set-ups where you can grab quick profits in a couple of days to a few weeks
• Laid back, patient, likes to take the long-term view, not easily riled	• Trend trading, using a moving-average approach to trading
• Hyper, tense, likes a lot of stimulation and fast action	• Day-trading approach, where you get in and out of the markets five to 20 times a day
• Meticulous, analytical, accountant mentality	• Point and figure, Elliott wave, regression analysis

break your success with a given type of system is simply your personality style.

Picking the right system for you requires having a solid handle on who you are. Table 5.1 matches the most effective trading strategies for different personality types.

The best way to select a trading system is to figure out what fits you and your psychological profile. Which system will you be most likely to stick to, and be most comfortable with, particularly when the markets turn against you? Which approach will enable you to remember you are playing with real money? Which one will help you preserve your psychological capital? Which system do you like? Again, a good contact for finding out about top trading systems is John Hill of Futures Truth Company (815 Hillside Road, Hendersonville, NC 28791; 828-697-0273). Hill has been trading futures for about 40 years. He has spent more than a dozen years rigorously testing dozens of technical systems and he is one of the leading authorities on trading system performance.

Any proven trading strategy or system is not inherently better than any other. Not all systems will work even with the best of traders. However, perhaps the key ingredient of a proven, profitable system is simply the degree to which a trader is willing to stick to it. If you approach trading or investing as a business, with profits and losses, and you execute a fundamentally sound business plan, you will tend to play the trading game correctly. As a result, you will reap financial capital and preserve psychological capital. Making trades is no different from making sales calls. A certain number of sales calls are successful, and many are a no-sale. Maintaining this perspective will keep you focused on your trading objectives and minimize the damage to your psychological capital when you have those unfortunate experiences known as losses.

CUSTOMIZE YOUR TRADING SYSTEM

Experienced, successful golfers wouldn't feel comfortable using someone else's clubs. They carefully select their own clubs, trying out steel and titanium, different lengths, and different-sized heads. The "right" clubs will feel right. They'll fit. The same is true for all the high-tech gizmos, such as laser range finders, which are used to pinpoint the exact distance from the fairway to the pin. Two equally talented golfers may prefer different bells and whistles. Similarly, it's difficult to trade someone else's system successfully, at least exactly as is.

For instance, there is real benefit to following Elliott wave theory in analyzing markets, as there is in following point and figure work and regression analysis. But candidly, for whatever reason, they don't trigger for me that intuitive feel for the markets that other indicators do. This may not be true for other traders—say, engineers, who are more mechanically oriented than I am.

Once you select a category of trading that suits your personality style and traits, you need to select a mix of market indicators that will make you the most comfortable, confident, and competent. Try out indicators for about 90 days and see if you ʋorking with them. Do they trigger a better feel, an intuitive sense of the market? Which ones give you a trader's edge? Which ones turn you into an artist, in *The Art of the Trade?*

At one time, my toolbox contained 77 technical indicators. It required a lot of work to follow that many indicators, and I found I got lost in them. I was overloaded. So I mixed and matched them, and whittled them down until I came up with a set of indicators that work best for me. Here are the main technical indicators I follow today, with descriptions adapted from CQG, Inc. and *Technical Analysis of Stocks & Commodities* materials.

ABC Elliott wave terminology for a three-wave countertrend price movement. Wave A is the first price wave against the trend of the market. Wave B is a corrective wave to A. Wave C is the final price move to complete the countertrend price move. Elliott wave followers study A and C waves for price ratios based on numbers from the **Fibonacci** series.

accumulation/distribution line If the current close is higher than the previous close, add the absolute value of the difference between the current close and the true low (the lesser of the current low or the previous close). If the current close is lower than the previous close, subtract the absolute value of the difference between the current close and the true high (the greater of the current high or the previous close). If the current close is equal to the previous close, the cumulative total is unchanged.

advance/decline line Each day's number of declining issues is subtracted from the number of advancing issues. The net difference is added to a running sum if the difference is positive, or subtracted from the running sum if the difference is negative.

average directional movement index (ADX) A derivative of the **DMI**, ADX measures the strength of a market trend, not its direction. The higher the ADX, the more directional the market has been (the stronger the trend). The lower the ADX, the less directional the market has been (the weaker the trend).

candlestick chart Plots highs and lows (referred to as shadows) as a single line. The price range (referred to as the body) between the open and the close is plotted as a narrow rectangle. If the close is above the open, the body is white. If the close is below the open, the body is black (see Figure 5.1). Candlestick charts originated in Japan.

channel Plots two lines as an overlay on the bar chart, which respectively identify the highest high and lowest low that occurred during a preceding period. There are three basic ways to draw channels: parallel, rounded, and connecting lows or highs. A channel is used to define a trading range—points that are expected to provide support and resistance. A move

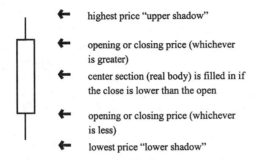

← highest price "upper shadow"

← opening or closing price (whichever is greater)

← center section (real body) is filled in if the close is lower than the open

← opening or closing price (whichever is less)

← lowest price "lower shadow"

Source: Commodity Quote Graphics

FIGURE 5-1 Candlestick chart

above or below the channel values may be considered a breakout from the trading range.

continuation chart   A chart in which the price scale for the data for the end of a given contract and the data for the beginning of the next contract are merged in order to ease the transition of one contract to the next in the futures market.

demand index   An index of the buying and selling power of markets and stocks, is determined by mathematical calculations of volume and price ratios.

directional movement index (DMI)   Developed by J. Welles Wilder, Jr., DMI measures market trend on a scale of 0 to 100. If you use a trend-following method, you would trade only those markets in the upper end of the scale; if you use a system that capitalizes on choppy or nontrending markets, you would trade only those markets at the lower end of the scale. DMI defines the equilibrium point, where directional movement up is in equilibrium with directional movement down.

Elliott wave theory   Published by Ralph Nelson Elliott in 1939, this pattern-recognition technique holds that the stock market follows a rhythm or pattern of five waves up and three waves down (a "correction" of the preceding five up) to form a complete cycle of eight waves.

fast stochastic   A pair of moving averages that measures, on a scale of 0 to 100, whether a market is overbought or oversold. The first line (the %K value) for each day is derived by subtracting the lowest low from the current price, then dividing the difference by the range (the highest high minus the lowest low). The %D value averages the %K value over a certain period of time to smooth out inconsequential market movement, to reveal the true, underlying trend. When the lines exceed 75, the market is considered overbought; when the lines dip below 25, the market is considered oversold. When the %K and %D lines cross, it usually indicates a change in short-term price direction.

Fibonacci ratio   The ratio between any two successive numbers in the Fibonacci sequence, known as *ph* (*f*). The ratio of any number to the next higher number is approximately 0.618 (known as the **golden mean** or **golden ratio**), and to the next lower number is approximately 1.618 (the inverse of the golden mean), after the first four numbers of the series. Three important ratios that the series provide are 0.618, 1.0, and 1.618.

fractals   Mathematical models that may be applied to identify data patterns.

fundamentals   The theory that stock and futures market activity may be predicted by looking at the relative data and statistics of a stock or commodity as well as the management of a company and its earnings.

Gann theory   Various trading techniques developed by the legendary trader W.D. Gann.

golden mean or golden ratio   The ratio of any two consecutive numbers in the Fibonacci sequence, equal to 0.618; an important proportion that is a phenomenon in music, art, architecture, and biology.

momentum indicator   A market indicator utilizing price and volume statistics for predicting the strength or weakness of a current market, and any overbought or oversold conditions, and to note turning points within the market.

moving average   A mathematical procedure to smooth or eliminate data fluctuations and to assist in determining when to buy and sell in a market. Moving averages emphasize the direction of a trend, confirm trend reversals, and smooth price and volume fluctuations that can confuse interpretation of the market; they represent the sum of a value plus a selected number of previous values divided by the total number of values. There are various types of weighted moving averages, with the 3-, 9-, and 21-day moving averages of closing prices being among the most popular.

multiple linear regression   More than one independent variable used to account for variability in one dependent variable.

on-balance volume (OBV)   Plotted as a line representing the cumulative total of volume. The volume from a day's trading with a higher close when compared with the previous day is assigned a positive value, whereas volume on a lower close from the previous day is assigned a negative value. Traders look for a confirmation of a trend in OBV with the market or a divergence between the two as an indication of a potential reversal.

open interest   Measures how many people are involved in a futures market on both the long side and short side. It is often a good indication of liquidity, how large a trading position you can have in the market, and whether you can expect reasonable executions on entries and exits. It tells you if the odds are good that any time you want to get in or out of a market, you'll be forced to feed positions into the market rather than liquidate them all at once. This is similar to looking at the number of a company's shares outstanding in the stock market. You want liquidity in the markets. Open interest is to be used in conjunction with **volume**.

oscillator   Identifies overbought and oversold price regions and plots the difference between two moving averages of different lengths or types. The difference between two moving averages with different sensitivities to market action provides an indication of the development of a change in the market environment, such as the emergence of a new trend or a trend reversal.

overbought/oversold indicator   Defines when prices have moved too far and too fast in either direction and thus are vulnerable to a new reaction

parabolic   A time/price reversal system created by J. Welles Wilder, Jr., used to follow trends by calculating the stop and reverse (SAR). A position is reversed when the protective stop loss is hit. As prices trend higher, the SARs tend to start out slower and then accelerate with the trend. In a down trend, the same thing happens, but in the opposite direction.

Pareto's law   States that 80 percent of results come from 20 percent of effort.

point and figure chart   A prices-only chart that plots up prices as Xs and down prices as Os. The minimum price recorded is called the box size. Typically, a three-box reversal indicates a change in the direction of prices.

relative strength index (RSI)   A price momentum indicator invented by J. Welles Wilder, Jr., to ascertain overbought or oversold situations. It is calculated by using the following formula:

$$RSI = 100 - [100 / (1 + RS)]$$

RS is the ratio of the exponentially smoothed moving average of n-period gains divided by the absolute value (i.e., ignoring sign) of the exponentially smoothed moving average of n-period losses. An RSI above 70 indicates an overbought condition; an RSI below 30 indicates an oversold condition.

reverse exponential moving average (REMA)   An average computed by working backward through the time series, rather than forward, as is the case with a standard **EMA**. A REMA is used so the target would reflect only future price behavior, not past action that would induce spurious correlation.

slow stochastic   A pair of moving averages of the **fast stochastic.** The slow %K equals the fast %D. The slow %D is an average of the slow %K. As with the fast stochastic, when the two slow stochastic lines cross, it indicates a change in the direction of short-term prices.

trading bands   Lines plotted in and around the price structure to form an envelope, answering whether prices are high or low on a relative basis and forewarning whether to buy or sell by using indicators to confirm price action.

trading range   The difference between high and low prices traded during a period. In a specific futures market it represents the high/low price limit established by the exchange for any one day's trading.

trendline   A line that connects a series of either highs or lows in a trend. It indicates a persistent change in price, either upward or downward. In an up trend, the lower limits of the fluctuation tend to form a straight line. In a down trend, the upper limits tend to conform to a straight line.

volume   The number of shares or contracts traded on a particular day. This is the pulse, the lifeblood, of the market that tells you how many people have come to the party. If you're trend or swing trading and prices are going up on increasing volume, it's a healthy market. Then, if volume spikes higher, this might be a sign of exhaustion. Or if the price continues to rise sluggishly on low volume, this may indicate the top of the market. When a market is going down, if you're on the short side, you want the price drop to occur on increasing volume. A huge spike in volume, though, may indicate exhaustion in selling. If volume drops off significantly and dries up, with sluggish price movement, you may be close to a trading bottom.

Williams' %R   An overbought and oversold indicator that is used to determine market entry and exit points. The system identifies the highest high and lowest low as well as the current price for a specified period. It subtracts the lowest low from the current price, then divides the difference by the range (where the range is the highest high minus the lowest low). The result is %R, which is identical to the fast stochastic %K line.

In addition to the technical indicators above, I follow several timing indicators, including:

cycle   Variation where a point of observation returns to its origin.
turning point   Time at which there is a change in trend.

I also pay close attention to sentiment indicators from *Bullish Consensus* and *Consensus* magazine to learn what percentage of investment advisers are bullish. I use the 80/20 rule to decide when the market is overbought or oversold. When less than 20 percent of advisers are bullish, that means more than 80 percent are bearish and the market has an 80 percent probability of reversing trend to the upside and a 20 percent probability of accelerating down. When a market is over 80 percent bullish, it means it has an 80 percent probability of reversing down and a 20 percent probability of accelerating up. Consolidation at these overbought and oversold levels favor the present trend direction.

LISTEN TO FUNDAMENTAL SIGNALS

Often fundamental factors in a particular market do not lend themselves to a given trading system. Twenty-five years ago, most traders followed fundamental trading systems. Today, however, the vast majority of traders use technical trading systems. Technical traders forget that there can be overriding fundamental factors that affect markets and can swamp all other technical, timing, and sentiment indicators. Being able to identify these key fundamental factors can make a tremendous difference in a trader's ability to trade successfully. Here is where *The Art of the Trade* comes into play.

I track fundamentals by reading the financial press and wire services such as Futures World News provided by CQG (especially the fundamental news summaries, FWN's daily market write-up for each particular market, and factors influencing the market that particular day) and Bloomberg, and by surfing the Internet. Good overall printed sources include *The Economist, Forbes, Business Week, Journal of Commerce, Wall Street Journal, Investor's Business Daily, London Times, International Herald Tribune,* and *Barron's.* I also monitor CNBC and *Wall Street Week.* I look for significant news concerning each market I follow, to get a sense of what the market's all about. I ask, "What are the primary, fundamental factors influencing a market?" This helps me develop my own trend expectations. It comes from what I know and learn about a market fundamentally, and the major factors in that market that impact price.

For instance, factors that are currently affecting the value of the Japanese yen include the new Japanese prime minister's economic programs, Japanese bank loans, how many Japanese banks are insolvent, how many examiners are available to review Japanese banks, Japanese consumer confidence, business sentiment, Japanese holdings and disposition of U.S. Treasury debt, and Japanese imports and exports. I watch the yen closely. If it dips for long below 150 to dollar, I suspect the negative impact on the Chinese yuan and the Hong Kong dollar could trigger a crisis in the international banking system.

Or, say you are following July coffee. You want to watch for a Brazilian freeze threat or an actual freeze, which would dramatically affect the July coffee price. Then, when the coffee market can no longer go higher on extremely positive price news (a freeze), it's often on top. (When a market no longer moves lower on extremely negative news, it is often on bottom.)

The fundamental expectation will also tell you that when a market doesn't do what you expect it to do in light of the news, this is often a tremendous opportunity to profit from a trade in the opposite direction. Also, there may be a significant factor out there that is unknown, that's overriding normal probability expectations. For example, if a freeze is not expected in Brazil, but the coffee price moves up in a strong technical fashion anyway, perhaps producers are withholding coffee from the market to strengthen the price, and that news is not in the market yet. Or perhaps there is some type of coffee disease that is reducing coffee crop size and boosting price.

As Figure 5.2 illustrates, fortunes were made on the 1994 and 1997 rallies in coffee. The 1994 rally was due to a freeze threat.

The general fundamental categories I track are weather, warfare, world trade, oil, inflation, interest rates, the U.S. dollar, and the Federal Reserve's approach to the money supply (restrictive or expansive). I follow monthly reports of who owns what—such as the percentage of positions that are held by commercials (like big cattle slaughterhouses in the cattle market, Johnson Mathey in platinum, or Cargill in grains), and the percentage of positions held by large and small speculators. Other important indicators include cash activity in various commodities markets, earnings reports of corporations, insider sales, solar and geophysical data from the National Oceanic and Atmospheric Administration, central bank gold sales, IMF funding recipients, Bank of International Settlements activity, USDA crop production reports, and cattle-on-feed reports. There are many, many fundamentals. There is no substitute, in my opinion, for the foundational base that can be established from a solid understanding of the fundamentals that affect a market.

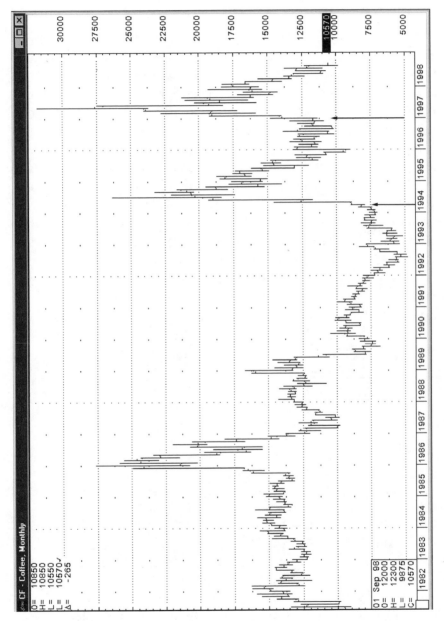

FIGURE 5-2 Rallies in coffee prices (Copyright 1998 CQG, Inc.) Fortunes were made on the 1994 and 1997 rallies in coffee. The 1994 rally was a freeze threat rally.

> Buy on rumor, sell on news.

How else do you weigh fundamental factors against technical, timing, and sentiment indicators? The fundamentals often give you confidence to stick with the trend if you're trading longer term. A market will tend to move with emerging fundamentals. However, once the news is known and in the market, normally there's good reason to at least take some profits short term. It's often wise to buy on rumor and sell on the announcement of fundamental news. Buy on the rumor of a freeze in Brazil. Then, once the price has already spiked higher and the freeze is announced, you'll probably want to sell because the market has likely already discounted the news by moving up in anticipation of the announcement. By the time an event becomes general news, the smart money has pretty well been made. Newcomers probably won't make a whole lot of money at that point. They may, in fact, lose. Remember, you make money only when there is risk, unknowns, uncertainty in the market.

As I wrote in my book *The Christ Within: The Church and New Age Seek Him* (A.N. Inc. International, 1995):

> Why do bankers often lose so much money making real estate loans? Because they really don't want to take any risks. They tend to wait until all the information is available and then they are willing to loan money. Well, when everything is known about something, then the risk is not there. If the risk is not there, the reward is not there. So, any time we know everything about an investment—it's on the front page of the *Wall Street Journal* or on the cover of *Time* magazine or *U.S. News & World Report*—it's time to be careful. . . . Who makes money in society? Those who take risks, the entrepreneurs. It's only with risk, stemming from faith, looking forward to the future, that prosperity and progress come. If we instead emphasize approval, control, and especially security in the seen world, what happens? We fall behind. We stagnate and decay. Life is progressive.

Once the news is known and the risk is removed, there is little profit potential left. But this does not mean you necessarily want to reverse positions. If a market has a head of steam, let it blow itself off. This is why it's important never to stand in the way of a runaway market. Even in my turning-point work, I wait for technical confirmation of hints of a trend change or a turn in momentum before positioning in opposition to the present trend. This gives me something to hang my hat on.

A good example occurred during the first half of 1998, when there were numerous oversold technical buy signals in the Japanese yen. But these technical signals were neutralized by the overwhelmingly negative economic fundamentals of the Japanese economy, which resulted in continued hammering of the yen. Despite the fact that sentiment indicators revealed that well over 80 percent of traders were pessimistic toward the yen and technical indicators showed that the market was consistently extremely oversold, the value of the yen continued to drop. Figure 5.3 shows only one contrary opinion rally worth playing from the long side in nearly three years (2nd quarter 1997).

The story was the same with copper. Because of a lack of demand for copper coming out of Asia, traders stayed extremely bearish in early 1998, excessively so technically, and in terms of market sentiment. Yet the price of copper continued to decline with no significant trading bounces. Oversold buy signals didn't mean a thing. At such times, it's important to ask yourself if there is something else going on. Is a fundamental factor affecting the market so powerfully that it invalidates normal timing, technical, and sentiment indicators? This can often be the case, contrarily so, now that the vast majority of traders trade exclusively technically. Figure 5.4 shows how copper prices collapsed from the second quarter of 1997 through the end of that year with no meaningful oversold rallies.

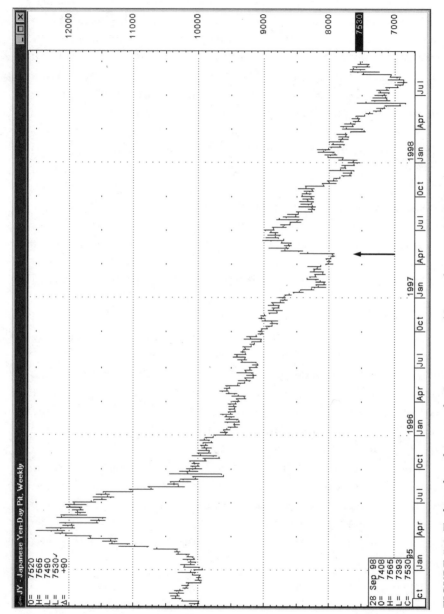

FIGURE 5-3 Technical weakness in the Japanese yen (Copyright 1998 CQG, Inc.)

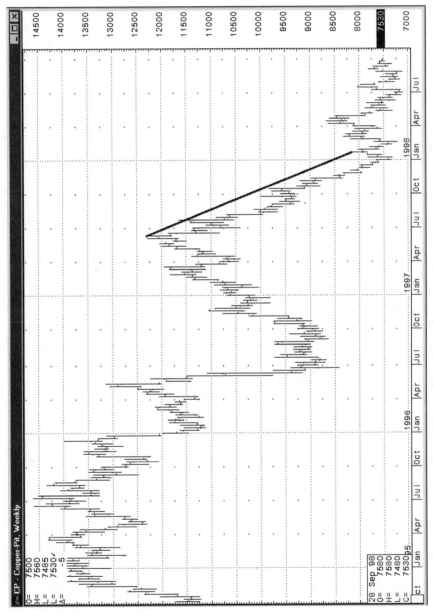

FIGURE 5-4 Copper price collapse (Copyright 1998 CQG, Inc.)

KNOW THE LIMITS OF YOUR TRADING SYSTEM

In both examples above, the markets were clearly trending downward with a powerful bias. It was clear they were not going to swing. If you use a swing-trading system that relies on buying oversold markets and then selling overbought markets, your technical indicators would be only marginally effective in the above two examples. Oversold buy signals triggered by stochastic indicators and relative strength indicators will lead to frustrating losses in powerful, fundamentally driven down trends. Trend traders would do better in this scenario. But if your personality traits indicate you would not make a good trend trader, you have two options. You can wait on the sidelines for occasional rallies into resistance to sell short. Or you can turn to other markets that are more favorably positioned for swing trading.

Whatever system you use, make sure you test it against today's market reality. To this day, many traders study—and use— the trading theories of W. D. Gann, a prominent trader during the first half of the twentieth century. His methodology, however, is seriously flawed in that it focuses on the price-weighted Dow Jones Industrial Average, and does not account for future stock splits. Gann theory basically attempts to pinpoint the best time to buy and sell by identifying major and minor market trends, and where changes will happen. Ken Fisher, in *One Hundred Minds That Made the Market* (Business Classics, 1994) wrote:

> Few aggressive traders haven't studied Gann, and while the realm of Gann devotees is not limited to quacks, almost every quack I've ever seen has Gann in his quiver of quackisms. While Gann's mathematical methodologies are quite primitive by modern computer-driven standards, they still feel good to the trader who works with paper, pencil, and calculator and wants to follow only a relatively few number of indicators. They are particularly exotic and mystical to those looking for a magic key to unlock the wealth of Wall Street—and there is never a shortage of people looking for just that.

DON'T TRADE ALONE

Recognize that we are all social creatures. We all have a need for love and acceptance, approval and recognition, in addition to the need for money and material things. How do you bring these two basic needs into balance? There is a verse in the Bible that says, "As iron sharpens iron, so does a man sharpen the countenance of a friend." Countenance refers to the electromagnetic field that you emit as the reflection of what's going on inside you; the Eastern religions call this the aura. Your socializing, your interactions, your nurturing with your fellow beings help build the psychological capital reflected in your aura. We need each other. This need has to be balanced with the need to stand individually in our trading decisions.

This brings us to a basic question with which philosophers have struggled over the centuries: How do we balance the rights of the individual with the rights of the collective? It is historically known as "the one and the many" question. The "many" are the individuals; the "one" is the collective. The dichotomy can also be captured as the trees and the forest, the parts and the whole, diversity creating unity, yang creating yin.

In terms of business and in life, the win-win-win technique is the way to optimize individual needs, the collective need, and the needs of the environment; to do this you must take the long-term view. You serve (give) before you receive, and as a by-product of serving (doing something) correctly, you are paid. Those you serve provide both your financial sustenance (money) and approval (love), because you have met their needs. That's the only way, ultimately, all can win. The approach brings a resolution to conflict in the economic marketplace, where situations are often considered dog-eat-dog and win-lose.

As I wrote in *The Christ Within:*

> On the old TV series *Dallas,* the character of J. R. Ewing was a rascal if there ever was one. Certainly, he believed in the win-lose philosophy, and the conflict-oriented, survival-of-the-fittest, evolutionary standard that sadly undergirds much of Western civilization today. Remember, it is

not conflict that brings about prosperity; it's cooperation contracting in the marketplace that brings about prosperity. If conflict brought about prosperity, all of us would be rushing to invest in Iraq and Lebanon, or maybe North Korea or Bosnia. But money flows to where there's peace and harmony so there can be a cooperative exchange of goods and services, and people can network.

There is something very detrimental about the futures markets because of their drawdown on psychological capital in a zero-sum game. They are win-lose. Again, two basic needs are to have both approval (love) and financial capital (money), but this drawdown in the futures markets takes its toll, and that doesn't occur in the normal capitalistic environment of the business world.

It is a myth that we are self-contained—each of us a rock, an island. Such attitudes devastate psychological capital. Eventually, as our psychological capital is drawn down, our financial capital is drawn down. One of the realities that came out of POW camps is that as the body's mineralization or physical reserve are depleted, and as psychological reserves are drawn down, a soldier's will is broken. So physical, financial, and psychological capital are inescapably interrelated in the battle of the markets.

There have been some great traders who were loners, who were brilliantly successful for periods of time, and who came to tragic ends. Like flaming comets, they burned out. Some committed suicide. The demands of the market are so extreme, you need to have support from someone, somewhere, to sustain the challenge of trading long term.

Trading, particularly in futures, tends to be a tough, lonely profession. It's a zero-sum, win-lose game that's highly leveraged, whose commercial interests know the important fundamentals and have an edge. Most of the time, you are seeking to break from the public trading crowd and take a contrarian position that will give you an edge over the rest of the pack. The following might help you keep your bearings. If you know where you stand in a market's life cycle, you can trade more prudently. As Figure 5.5 shows, a bull market normally has three legs up:

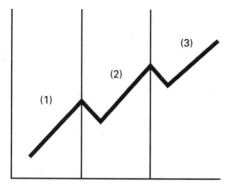

oversold   fairly valued   overbought

FIGURE 5-5 Three legs of an up trend

(1) when it is oversold and undervalued, (2) as it becomes fairly valued, and (3) when it becomes overvalued. Normally, the masses of traders are correct only in the middle third of that upward move, leg 2. They don't catch the market at the bottom when it is oversold, and then they tend to hang on too long in the overvalued leg, causing them to give back much of their profits. As trend followers, they are usually correct only in the middle leg, which is the only time it's okay to be part of the crowd. The rest of the time, you need to stand on your own two feet, buy on fear at the bottom (undervalued), when little positive is known, and sell on greed at the top (overvalued). Ideally, therefore, you trade comfortably with the masses (or the funds) only about one-third of the time.

So how do you find that delicate balance between your love (people) needs and your need to stand alone as a trader to optimize making money? You must first recognize this reality and bring it up to your level of consciousness so you'll know it exists, and know how to deal with it. The trick, then, is to seek the company of other traders and colleagues to bounce around market ideas, to listen to their concepts, and to gather emotional support. That doesn't mean you need to agree with them or judge them; nor does it mean you have to trade reclusively, huddled in a corner.

I have found that trading with someone who shares my interests and is emotionally supportive tends to bring me into balance. If I try to trade long term just by myself, I may do well for a while, but the drawdown in psychological capital sooner or later takes its toll. Besides, I find it boring and unfulfilling just to make money on my own.

Maybe you trade by yourself and have your social and psychological support group outside the marketplace. In any case, there has to be some way to nurture and rebuild your psychological capital from the drawdown that takes place, particularly in the futures trading arena, if you are going to survive long term. Maybe you need to do something beneficial, such as give part of your profits to charity. After all, you do still reap what you sow, and electromagnetically you get back what you give off. What goes around comes around. Make no mistake about it, there is truth to reaping what you sow, and to karma. As you will see in Chapter 7, you are a walking infrared antenna; you're broadcasting your own frequencies all the time. As such, you will tend to attract back whatever you're broadcasting. So it is important for you to maintain an interpersonal balance with your psychological capital. You need support and support systems. Put differently, you need people with whom you can celebrate the good times and who will grieve and cry with you when you are down and out, who will encourage you to get up and to move forward. You want people in your life who are synergistic, who add to your life as you add to theirs, where the whole is greater than the sum of the parts. You want to cut your losses short and avoid people who are drawdowns on your psychological capital.

In summary, what do we watch out for? A complementary perspective comes from David Hightower, an expert analyst of markets and traders, who is a principal of Hartfield Management, Inc. in Chicago and is editor of *The Hightower Report* (800-662-9346). He lists a dozen reasons why traders fail:

1. They have inadequate capitalization.
2. They are using someone else's system.
3. They lack knowledge of the system's performance.

4. They are unable to sit through flat periods or drawdowns.
5. They are unable to handle stress.
6. They lack commitment.
7. They experience drawdowns that are greater than their hypothetical testing.
8. They override the system's signals.
9. Their ego prevails.
10. The system is overoptimized; they make additional rules to take out losing trades.
11. They lack parameters for spike performance in markets.
12. They lack diversification between systems and/or markets.

THE CONSISTENCY OF THE TRADE

Now that you have worked on selecting a trading system that fits your personality, and have selected technical, timing, sentiment, and fundamental indicators to follow, you must focus on figuring out how you will implement your trading system consistently.

We are all affected by what goes on around us, by our environment, and by the people with whom we interface. Having these external factors in harmony with your needs in order to trade successfully is just as important as doing all your key internal and analytical work. Although not discussed very often, a measure of consistency is critical to an investor's success.

Consistency is your willingness to put trading first in your life so you're online day in and day out, trading your system to maximize the odds that it will work for you when the market is moving. When traders take a break for whatever reason—because they want to play, because they have experienced a series of losses, because of complications in their personal lives, or because the market is dead—they end up missing moves that could have resulted in hefty profits. In my own trading career, time and time again, I have found that it is my willingness and discipline to put the markets first that is the key to having the odds work in my favor. When the markets are quiet or you have a series of losses, or a number of pressing personal demands, it is easy to get discouraged and goof off, or divert your attention to some other endeavor. Inevitably, that's when you'll miss one of those really big winning trades.

That doesn't mean you always have to trade, but you should always be there to follow the markets. In fact, if your personal life is unsettled, you should usually reconsider trading. Traders tend to lose more money trading when their personal lives are unsettled, whether because of a divorce, problems with a son or daughter, a health situation, or the death of a parent. If your personal life is devastated, you need to work through it and then get back to the markets. You must be at peace with yourself, your environment, your fellow citizens, and your family to be able to focus and clearly discern what's going on in the markets.

Four key principles of balance that bring a measure of consistency to life are humility, responsibility, empathy, and duty. Humility and responsibility are internal, individual traits you must handle personally. Empathy and duty are external, and have to do with your response to the collective—other people.

Take, for instance, our automobile traffic system. All of us go around driving 50 to 60 miles an hour in 2000-pound behemoths, which are potential killing machines. Yet we have this fascinating, nearly collision-free collective movement of traffic. Why? The collective is created by individuals who operate according to the principles of humility, responsibility, empathy, and duty in what is potentially a very dangerous environment. Unless we all drive with humility, empathy, responsibility, and duty, following the rules of the road, our marvelous traffic system will not function. It doesn't matter what culture we're in or what religion we profess either. Look at the automobile traffic systems everywhere in the world—Korea, Singapore, China, Nigeria, Panama, Mexico, Argentina, Europe, the United States. When they function properly, all operate according to these four principles, which balance out the needs of the individual with the needs of the collective to bring the system into harmony.

HUMILITY

Each individual driver, to the degree he or she is willing be humbled to the rules of the road, enables the whole traffic system to run harmoniously. Everyone then has freedom and safety, and traffic movement is maximized. To the degree that individuals do not function within those rules, do not humble themselves, the system will not operate in a safe, efficient manner. Every driver is expected to demonstrate the humility to yield to the authority of those traffic rules (e.g., a stop sign). A traffic cop is not always looking over your shoulder to make sure you do so; it takes humility not to be lawless and instead to put yourself under the authority of the traffic laws. Humility demonstrates respect for the system and a willingness to put something else above yourself as a final authority.

It takes humility for traders to submit themselves to the trading boundaries: the authority of the rules of trading in the exchange and the limitations your broker puts on you. It takes humility to yield to the market and flow (trade) with it.

RESPONSIBILITY

It takes responsibility to know what you should do and to do it. In the auto traffic system, you must have a sense of what's right and wrong. A responsible driver will drive safely and obey the rules of the road, whether a police officer is in sight or whether a parent is in the back seat nagging at them to slow down, to drive more cautiously in dangerous road conditions. A responsible driver drives in the correct lane at the speed limit.

It takes responsibility for traders to recognize that only if everyone follows the rules laid down for trading, particularly given the verbal contracts, will the markets function efficiently, accurately reflect supply and demand, act somewhat predictably, and come back to value, leading to opportunities to profit.

EMPATHY

Empathy flows from responsibility. There is a mutual contract with other drivers. Just as you are willing to respect the rules of the road to maximize others' freedom and safety, so you expect others to do as well for you. Irresponsible drivers, such as those who drive under the influence of alcohol, endanger not only themselves but others as well. They are irresponsible partly because they lack empathy for those they endanger. People with empathy see past their own needs and comfort. They are concerned with the welfare of their fellow citizens.

It takes empathy to appreciate the purpose of brokers, exchange members, and regulatory authorities, to respect the fact that they serve a useful purpose and need to make a living. Empathy also enables you to understand what other traders and players in the market are thinking, waiting, hoping, and needing. Empathy opens you up to what might happen next, which provides a key to understanding the flow of the market. The ability to think not only from your own perspective, but from someone else's, is what gives you an edge, an opportunity to profit. Like a good chess player, you will be able to think about two different strategies simultaneously.

The opposite of humility and empathy is pride and selfishness, which can severely restrict you from thinking beyond your own limited perspective. The more you have empathy and understand the other side of the market, the greater your feel will be for how the market is moving. Empathy increases the probability that you'll be able to trade successfully, whatever direction the market is moving.

DUTY

Duty is a vital peg in terms of how this perspective manifests toward others. Duty has to do with ethics, with following two rules that exist in all religions:

1. Keep your word and honor your commitments (the basis of contract law).
2. Don't violate or trespass on other people or their property (the basis of criminal and some tort law).

You have a duty to perform according to your implied contracts. If you're a wheat farmer who sold a contract to deliver

5000 bushels of wheat, you have a duty to deliver that wheat. To the degree that people agree to meet their duties by fulfilling their contracts, the markets will maximize everyone's interests long term.

The trading market, in essence, involves many implied contracts, where people's word is their bond. A contract, by definition, is a moral, legal, and economic document. It is moral because it is no better than the character of the parties to the contract. It is legal because its provisions are binding and enforceable according to the rule of law. It is economic because it lays out the benefits and sanctions for fulfilling and not fulfilling the contract. Traders are creating a contract when they place an order with their broker. If they don't honor a margin call or if the broker does not fill the trade in an ethical way (by putting personal orders in ahead of the client's, for example), it causes problems in the system.

If you integrate these four principles—humility, responsibility, empathy, and duty—into your personal life, your professional life will become a lot more settled as well. As a result, your psychological capital will be enhanced and your ability to trade consistently and profitably will improve.

TREATING TRADING AS A PROFESSION

Another measure of consistency is to recognize that you are self-employed. You are running your own business. Whether or not you have a regular job, you should approach trading as you would holding a job. If you miss a day of work for some flimsy reason, you could be fired, and might not have enough money to buy food for your family. If you approach trading in a business-like fashion, you will show up for work in the markets on a regular, daily basis. This takes a tremendous amount of discipline, character, and self-restraint. Why not stay in bed if you had a hard night? There are a million excuses not to go to work the next day. But the reality is, you are self-employed. Look at your responsibility to yourself, your family, and trading with the same commitment you would devote to a job or a business. You could not get away with goofing off on the job, so you shouldn't get away with it in your own trading business. It's very easy once you're self-employed and trading to excuse yourself for all kinds of reasons. This can prove to be a devastating mistake. You will find over time that those days you take off to play golf or go fishing or whatever will inevitably be the days when the two or three trades you've been waiting for are triggered. These trades would have made your month very profitable. Then you have to scramble for the rest of the month. When you trade this way, you tend to lose money. Inconsistency does not pay off.

To stay focused on the job, some traders get dressed up for work every day, even if they trade from their homes. This helps them stay professional. Then, at the end of the market day, they change their clothes and relax.

STALK THE TRADE LIKE A LION STALKS ITS PREY

When a lion first spots its prey, it instinctively analyzes the best strategy for capture. Then it moves through various tactical maneuvers to achieve that goal. Similarly, a good trade follows naturally from much preparation and a solid measure of consistency. In other words, you've done your homework the night before, you've slept on it; you get up early in the morning, and the market is moving in the way you expect it to move. You have psychological consistency; you can trade easily. The best trades move in an easy pattern from perception to implementation over time. This allows the trade to develop, to come together, to have its own flow. It allows all the analytical work you've done in the left brain to be complemented by the intuitive decision making of the right brain, where the real creative brilliance and excellence of trading can be achieved, fulfilling *The Art of the Trade.*

For instance, by the close of 1998, the fundamentals had begun to fall into place for a big bull market in protein gold (grain) in 1999 and 2000. The known fundamentals are bearish and already discounted by the market. Globally, we still have large grain stocks and sinking demand from the Asian economic depression and bountiful harvests. We have already gone through commodity deflation, with protein gold prices at or below Great Depression levels. We've had bankruptcies in agriculture, slumping exports, and excellent growing conditions in the United States. Prices have dropped and dropped and dropped some more. But weather-based emerging fundamentals over the upcoming two years are starting to turn bullish, and the market seems to be exhausting all these well-known, fleshed-out, bearish fundamentals.

So I'm beginning to stalk the protein gold market, putting on some exploratory long-term positions in protein gold in a market that's been beaten down by bearish negative fundamentals for so long that they could be about to be replaced by bullish fundamentals. Plus, if we get any type of return of inflation and a commodity bull market where a rising tide lifts all boats, a tremendous amount of money could be made on the long side of protein gold. A weather shift to La Niña could cause havoc in the protein gold growing belts internationally. So I'm watching the fundamentals, the weather, prices, and value, and am preparing to stalk my prey, some extremely undervalued long positions in protein gold.

This is not any different from what Warren Buffett uncharacteristically did when he bought silver in July 1997. Buffett is known for his desire to buy and hold for long periods of time. However, he spotted an enticing trading opportunity after the silver market was beaten down from $50 to $4 an ounce. He saw an opportunity to position on the long side of a market, where fundamental demand was exceeding supply consistently on an annual basis, silver was undervalued, and the market was demoralized. He looked at the emerging fundamentals, stalked the position, analyzed ongoing developments, stalked the silver market some more, and captured his prey. He bought up to 20 percent of the world's annual silver production, almost 130 million ounces, worth $860 million, perfectly timing his purchases beginning on July 25, 1997 at $4.32 an ounce. It paid off for him handsomely. (Incidentally, I told my clients to buy silver at the same time.)

If, by contrast, you trade on impulse, you'll likely dissipate not only psychological capital but also financial capital. Very few traders are gifted enough to be able to just get up in the morning, look at the markets, see an opportunity, and trade. Most of us are not so blessed. I find that the best long-term traders implement a plan in the markets that they prepared for days or weeks in advance and slept on the night before. The markets are moving consistently with their expectations.

This goes back to the basic life conflict of the urgent versus the important. Using Pareto's law again, 80 percent of the general population react to the urgent demands of life; they need structure and guidance outside of themselves to help them prioritize and channel their attention, energy, work, and efforts. These folks are always in crisis management, which burns up their psychological capital. That's the natural thing to do. Only 20 percent or less can really focus on doing the important things in life that entail planning, management, the long-term view, and being disciplined. At least 80 percent of people are reactive to stimuli rather than responsive to upcoming opportunities. The natural aristocrats—the wealthy, the capitalists, entrepreneurs, managers, the savers and investors in any society—take the long-term view. They are disciplined. They plan ahead and execute their plans consistently.

To bring additional consistency to your trading, you need to break away from the 80 percent and pattern the behavior of the natural aristocracy. You will be well served by becoming quieter, more grounded, responsive to stimuli and opportunities. You'll come from a more settled, well-reasoned place of balance. We have limited time, but tons of choices, responsibilities, and priorities that pull on us in our hectic world. A responsive, conscious, forward-looking approach helps us sort out all these competing alternatives. To maximize life (and trading), you must learn how to be comfortable with pain—the pain of constantly having to choose among many good alternatives and letting go of all the rest. This takes a mature, disciplined approach. It's much easier for most people to react to whatever grabs them at any particular time. This is the tyranny of the urgent. It's easy, for instance, for a single parent to get torn asunder by laundry, cooking, housekeeping, and car repairs, which forces the truly important thing—training the children—into second place. You can't ignore urgent things, but neither should you give yourself to them every time they scream at you, only to watch the important things in life slip by.

Day trading? Maybe occasionally, maybe for fun, maybe if there is an unusual opportunity. But be aware that day trading will dissipate psychological capital and reduce the number of years you will be able to trade the markets. It takes a tremendous amount of emotional and psychological capital to day-trade regularly.

The following poem points to the difficulty of staying focused and bringing consistency to trading when markets are volatile and unpredictable.

MODERN MARKETS

Markets come
Markets go
Money's made
By the ebb and flow.

Prices rise
Prices fall
The key's to survive
Through it all.

Gold is off
Stocks have soared
Paper gold
Has swept the floor.

Wheat's down
Utilities up
Microsoft stock
Bought many new pickups.

Money's the measure
Of everything
A higher DJIA
Makes hearts sing.

Cash is trash
Funds do rule
Easy money
Markets are cool.

Bubbled manias
All around
Everyone's
Out on the town.

NY or Chicago's
The place to be
Country bumpkins
Now Wall Street want-to-be's.

Farmers going
Belly up
While city folks
Live it up.

Cities prosper
The country withers
Basics swapped
For glitz and glitter.

THE MENTALITY OF THE TRADE

Making money, increasing financial capital, investing dollars, can be viewed as a left-brain analytical activity. At the same time, you want to balance your desire to make money by looking at the markets as a challenging way of having fun, of learning and growing, of having your right brain kick in. You want to be able to smile, whether you're winning or losing, so that you can be at peace and preserve psychological capital in the process.

LEFT AND RIGHT BRAIN IN HARMONY

Using your left-brain analytical system, you are in the markets to make money, not to be correct, not to build your ego. At the same time, it is beneficial to see the markets as a learning experience. What can you learn? What growing opportunities are available? Win, lose, or draw, there's always something to learn. If you keep this perspective in mind while trading the markets, your psychological capital will be better preserved; your financial capital will then have a greater opportunity to increase. If you minimize your errors, by practicing management by exception (as explained in Chapter 4), good things tend to happen. Profits take care of themselves as probabilities balance out

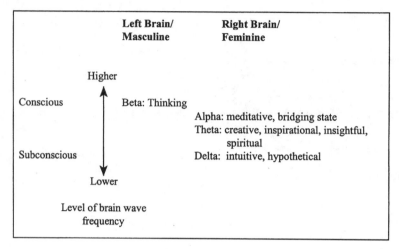

FIGURE 7.1   Aspects of the brain

longer term. Life is too short not to have fun doing whatever you do. If you don't enjoy trading, I recommend you don't do it.

THINKING IN GREEK WITH BETA, ALPHA, THETA, AND DELTA BRAIN WAVES

Your brain has four types of brain waves: delta, theta, alpha, and beta. Each has a different frequency and level of consciousness. For instance, as Figure 7.1 illustrates, the beta waves are a left-brain function that operates at a fairly high level of consciousness and emits a high-level frequency (actual, measurable in hertz [cycles per second]).

When your brain waves are fully active and integrated, when all four types are in harmonious frequency, you too are in harmony. You are able to think logically using the beta brain waves; you can think intuitively and hypothetically using the delta brain waves; you can be inspirational, have personal insight, and be spiritually aware using the theta brain waves; and, finally, you can experience the relaxed meditative, detached awareness provided by the alpha waves with their unusual bridging capacity.

LESSONS LEARNED FROM NEWTONIAN AND QUANTUM PHYSICS

In such an integrated state, your brain has the capacity to operate in space and time electromagnetically (in the Newtonian world of physics) and in time and space magnetoelectrically (in the holistic, supernatural world of quantum physics).

Imagine that we are standing at opposite ends of a 100-yard football field. One of us shines a light to the other end of the field and has that light reflect back off a mirror. It takes time for the rays to travel at the speed of light to hit the mirror 100 yards away and then be reflected back. That's linear, Newtonian physics. That's an electromagnetic activity occurring in time through space. It is what Eastern religions call yang—the masculine—which has to do with light, the left-brain, diversity, and individuality.

By contrast, if we hold up two magnets at different ends of that same football field, the magnetic fields are there instantaneously—as if they had been there all the time, in the collective, the one. That's what Eastern religions call the yin—the feminine—and science calls the magnetoelectric. It just exists. This is where intuition resides, in the great all-in-all, where limitless information is available. There is no time and space phenomenon here. It is beyond time and space.

As Tom Peters writes in *Liberation Management: Necessary Disorganization for the Nanosecond Nineties* (Knopf, 1992):

> We are so set in our ways that we fail to realize that there are robust mental frameworks that have stood the test of time, and that offer genuine, full-fledged alternatives to our normal modes of thought and conventional imagery. Frankly, it's hard to overestimate the degree to which we are subconsciously governed by old maps. When we Americans think strategy, often as not we think football. What a disaster! Football fields are circumscribed. Opponents show up at a set time to play. When a whistle blows, both sides stop. . . . Quantum mechanics is weird. I've read perhaps a dozen popular books on the topic. . . . Though originally trained as a

scientist, I understand little more about quantum mechanics than when I opened the cover of the first one. But I have been devastated and emotionally affected. It doesn't add up. And that, more or less, is the point.

Peters points out the implications of quantum mechanics on organization management. He notes that

> quantum mechanics, which has trumped Newtonian physics the way the car trumped the horse (horses were fine at the time and still have their place), is the best explanation we now have of the "physical" world. It's an explanation wholly at odds with the deterministic, Newtonian past. . . . [O]rganizational arrangements emerging in our highly interconnected, fast-paced, intangible/knowledge-intense, relationship-driven global village seem far more consistent with "quantum reality" than "Newtonian reality." Relationships. Networks. The intangibilizing ("informating") of everything. "Spiderweb" organizations. All these ideas are a piece with the elusive (key word!) principles of quantum physics.

There are equally valid and useful implications of these two models in the world of trading. You can operate in the familiar world of physical matter or in the spiritual, intuitive world. Ideally, you operate in both simultaneously when all brain waves are active and your brain is balanced. When all four brain waves are operating in sync, you can minimize stress in your life too. Certainly, trading is a stressful enough activity as it is. You can minimize stress when you process the events that come to you in life in a calm and peaceful way and keep your brain waves integrated. Otherwise, stress negatively impacts the brain's limbic system (associated with emotional expression, learning, and self-preservation) as well as the hypothalamus (a part of the limbic system that regulates emotional expression and visceral responses) and the pituitary gland or master gland (which commands the body to produce hormones by sending messages to the other glands, produces growth hormone, and regulates skeletal growth, blood pressure, and smooth muscle contractions).

So stress negatively impacts our endocrine system, our autonomic nervous system, and our immune system. The result may be gastrointestinal distress such as a peptic ulcer, adrenal overload leading to high blood pressure, poor metabolism, and/or a depressed immune system manifested by dysfunction of the thymus, spleen, lymph nodes, or outbreaks on the skin.

Renowned scientists in all fields have held that spirit—perfect living energy with personality, purpose, and information—should create perfect living matter. For instance:

- Robert O. Becker, M.D., in his books *The Body Electric: Electromagnetism and the Foundation of Life,* co-authored with Gary Seldon and Maria Guamaschelli (William Morrow, 1987), and *Cross Currents: The Promise of Electromedicine, the Perils of Electropollution* (J. P. Tarcher, 1991), confirmed that the human electrical field is the determinant of what occurs in the physical body.

- Harold Saxton Burr, M.D., a Yale University School of Medicine professor of anatomy and neuroanatomy and author of *Blueprint for Immortality: The Electric Patterns of Life* (N. Spearman, 1986), established that the L-field, the electrodynamic field, reveals the physical and mental conditions of the body and makes it possible for physicians to diagnose illnesses before the usual symptoms develop and are manifest in the physical body itself. After 40 years of documentation, Dr. Burr confirmed that all living things—plants, animals, and humans—are controlled by an electrodynamic field, which can be measured and mapped with standard modern voltmeters.

- Stanley Keleman reported in *Your Body Speaks Its Mind: The Bio-Energetic Way to Greater Emotional and Sexual Satisfaction* (Center Press, 1981) that the physical human body is a reflection of its mental and emotional processes.

- Lowell Ward, a chiropractor, worked with his son at Loma Linda Hospital in California. In conjunction with German physicians, they accumulated more than 30 years of documentation in mapping out with computers how the body reflects what is going on in the mind and the emotions.

Being fully conscious means having the delta, theta, alpha, and beta brain waves in sync, and also having the left brain and right brain harmonized, complemented by mental and emotional integrity. You want to be fully alive, aware, conscious, to live in the moment, in the now, not in the past or in the future. This is where you are able to bring everything you have to bear upon the reality with which you are dealing at any point in time. Who you are and who you perceive yourself to be need to be integrated if you are to respond best to the challenges of the market. You must be in reality and not in self-delusion. You should be in a relaxed, peaceful state that is not anxious or angry to function at maximum capacity.

When you are operating on the brain's left side, when you're thinking, you're in beta. This is the active, physical world of here and now, of sight, sound, smell, taste, and touch, of time and space. This is the conscious level. If you are not upset and you're able to settle down, the reality of the analytical work you do at this level harmonizes with the lower brain frequencies: alpha, theta, and delta. You do not want to be upset or angry, but instead relaxed so you can drop down into the meditative state of alpha; then further drop down into the creative, inspirational, aware, insightful state of theta; and next integrate with the intuitive delta waves of the brain. This is operating at full capacity brainwise. It gives you an incredible edge trading the market. It brings to the fore *The Art of the Trade.* It is a far cry from the frenzied state in which most traders operate.

OPTIMUM HEALTH LEADS TO OPTIMUM TRADING

You are not wealthy unless you are healthy, and there's a very slim chance of getting wealthy if you are unhealthy. This is particularly true in the arena of trading. Your health ultimately depends on your personal responsibility about how you think and feel, how you perceive and process the reality around you. If you are not at ease, you will be vulnerable to dis-ease. If you are constantly in a fight-or-flight mode, you are also in your Newtonian mode, and the stress this creates on the sympathetic nervous system in turn allows stress to creep into the parasympathetic, quantum side of your subconscious. Such stress contributes, among other things, to heart attacks.

Organs do communicate with each other. The spleen and pancreas communicate with the gall bladder and the liver in the process of digestion. So, in a real sense, you have to decide if you're going to be healthy. You can decide what you will think about. Emotions are a choice. You can choose to be at ease regardless of your circumstances. You then have the opportunity to become wealthy.

The immune system is a virtual second brain that remembers everything that has ever entered the body. The immune system distinguishes between friendly and unfriendly antigens and goes to battle against the unfriendly ones. There is an emerging medical field of psychoneuroimmunology, which has to do with how our brain and mind field works, how it affects our nerves, and in turn how it impacts our immune system.

Martin Rush, M.D., offered this observation in the August 1, 1998, issue of *Bottom Line*:

> Scientists have known for years that our emotions affect our bodies as well as our minds. When you feel angry, threatened, or upset, a series of physical changes is initiated by the hypothalmus—the area of the brain that is located on the underside of the cerebrum. The hypothalmus sends impulses to the adjacent pituitary gland. That in turn sends signals to the adrenal glands to release "stress chemicals," called catecholamines, into the bloodstream. These chemicals activate the nervous system. They make your blood pressure rise, your heart beat faster, your gut contract, and they make your hair stand on end.

Work done on human energy fields by Valerie Hunt, professor emeritus of the department of physiological sciences at the University of California at Los Angeles, confirms that the mind is a field that interacts with and surrounds the entire human body, not just the brain. Dr. Hunt has spent 25 years measuring and mapping human bioenergy, and she was the first researcher to make objective, repeatable measurements of the full spectrum of the field surrounding the human body. She was also the first to discover vibration patterns during pain, disease, and illness, and in emotional and spiritual states. Bringing together overlapping truths from many disciplines, Hunt has found scientific evidence of individualized field signatures and subtle energetic happenings between people and within groups.

In *Infinite Mind* (Malibu Publishing, 1996), Dr. Hunt writes:

> We know that reality is infinitely more complex than science has ever envisioned, even beyond any single religious ideology existing today. The extended concept of reality postulates an open system—where constant interactions and transactions take place back and forth between all existing systems—in contrast to the closed system of the past. Quantum physics has heralded its birth. The most profound changes in the conception of reality came from Einstein's Unified Field Theory. This theory states that all matter is organized energy, and that the field is in reality one of the characteristics of the universe. The deeper one probes material systems, the more one encounters field aspects of the substance's underlying electrical pattern, the very basis of the substance itself.

As I wrote in *The Christ Within:*

> Leading physicians today state that at least 80 percent of all disease has an emotional base. When we fail to handle the challenges of life properly, our emotions slow down below the speed of light and become living dark crystals in our bodies. These living dark crystals or biological resistors impede light/energy flow, shutting down geometric and holographic electromagnetic connections, which vent and feed down from the heavens through the head down to the feet, grounding in the earth, and feed from the earth up through our feet. The greater our number of bio-resistors, the less functional we are. . . . Unless the spirit, heart, soul, mental

and emotional software programming is changed, particularly down into the delta, theta, and alpha regions of the subconscious, the same old patterns will reemerge, maybe worse.

In an ideal state, you can let your analytical left brain serve as the foundation, the grounding platform from which the intuitive right brain can spring forth. You will always trade best when you are free to do so, when your insight from the right brain kicks in, unencumbered by internal and external distractions and pressures. All your left-brain work is simmering in a cauldron that allows the intuitive, right-brain insight to come forth. When all the ingredients are pulled together, you can "smell" and "taste" what is best to do in the market. This is synergy, the creation of a whole that is more than the sum of its parts. When the setup is complete, and when your intuition tells you to, you have the courage, capability, will, and ability to go against trading public opinion. You can let the correct decisions for trading unveil themselves at the proper time without forcing a decision. You are manifesting *The Art of the Trade*.

LEARNING TO STEP OUTSIDE YOURSELF

We all have the ability to delude ourselves. To trade (or do anything) successfully, you need to counteract your delusions. The more you are able to use your intuition, the more you will short-circuit your delusions to build self-confidence in your trading. If you can step outside yourself to observe your actions with impartiality, you will also have a better chance of knowing that the trading decision you are making is the best one. A good technique I know for stepping outside yourself is to imagine that there are expert consultants standing behind you, looking over your shoulder as you are about to make a trade. What would they tell you to do? Would they feel you are thinking objectively and following your trading system and money management plans? You may find it helpful to imagine a respected mentor standing behind you; others find it effective to imagine someone they are mentoring. For example, if your children were there with you, what would you tell them to do in the trade in question?

As you become more objective, you will find that the questions about major decisions you confront will come after a series of good small decisions. You will have more trust in your instinct, in your insight, and in your intuition for you have built a base of support. You will not feel threatened by those who disagree with you and take the other side of the trade. You will remain comfortable and secure in brainstorming sessions with other traders who challenge your perspective. At the same time, you will be able to take input from others that is useful and, if necessary, alter your position without feeling insecure. Pieces of the puzzle will just seem to fall into place.

In an ideal state, you can break out of preestablished procedures and traditional roles and do something new, intuitive, and creative with confidence. Eventually, this intuition will begin to feel like second nature. In times of crisis you will trust your intuition. It is better to have a trained intuition ahead of time rather than having to make a leap of faith in an emergency.

You will know who you are logically and intuitively, with left brain and right brain in sync, with all four brain rhythms in harmony, when you are fully conscious and living in the present, and are at peace. Left-brain analysis and right-brain intuition will kick in and work together. You will begin to find clues in a sea of low-weighted, seemingly insignificant facts that give you intuitive insight. When you know you have this insight, you can often go back to the left brain to justify it analytically. But you don't have to. You just "know" it.

For example, during President Clinton's mid-1998 visit to China, amid the crisis in the Nikkei Dow and the Japanese yen, I just intuitively knew we would have a trading bottom in the Nikkei Dow. It was like hearing a delicate whisper from across the room, something I normally do not pay attention to unless I am still, quiet, and integrated. I had a feeling that the market (Nikkei Dow) had been sold into a hole. The sentiment was excessively bearish, technical indicators were oversold, and the fundamentals were too bleak. I didn't see anything particularly bullish in that market—in fact, I couldn't justify my feeling. It turns out that June 15 was the exact day the September Nikkei Dow bottomed, at 14,520. Then it rallied to 16,780 on July 20 before again selling off (see Figure 7.2). It had looked like it was going to test and break the critical 14,000 support level and fall through the floor in mid-June. It was right there, but it didn't do it. Somehow, I just knew it wouldn't. And I followed my hunch. I did not have my pride at stake in being right or wrong; I was open to receiving the signal. There were no emotional or egotistical blocks. The only technical signal I could find to support my hunch was that the Nikkei Dow market was extremely oversold psychologically and technically. But I put myself in a position that was the equivalent of standing in the way of a runaway freight train at full speed. If I was wrong, I would have been crushed. So I paused for just a little confirmation, by waiting for the momentum to slow, followed by a minor reversal, and then I gave a buy signal to my clients. It turned out well.

The goal is to be able to analyze, synthesize experience, sense intuitively, and operate synergistically, to see and take advantage of the big picture. I know my brain waves are integrating well when I'm mountain biking, or when I wake up with new insights or answers that seem to come out of left field, when I'm not consciously thinking about a problem or a trade, when I have confidence to let my mind work in an open, freewheeling, unforced manner.

You can sharpen these intuitive skills by keeping a journal, as I recommend in Chapter 3. Write down all the questions and thoughts that come to mind and then review them on a regular basis. Because trading is not an exact science, but an art, you are dealing with the imperfect, the unknown, and that requires intuition to be successful long term. This means you must do the work on the basis of your experience, resources, explanation of options, and analysis of facts. Then let intuition take over. Sometimes the best decision is to do nothing, to not trade.

You want to get to the point where you do what seems to be the right thing. It just feels right. There is an easy flow to it. You shouldn't let conventional wisdom stifle your intuitive guidance. Ask God for help. Then you must trust your own inner

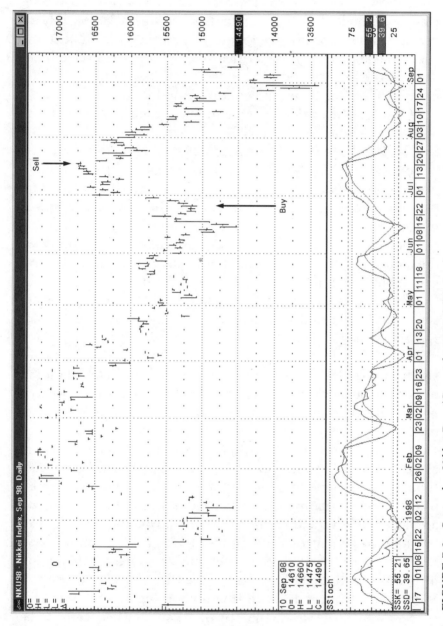

FIGURE 7.2 September Nikkei Dow (Copyright 1998 CQG, Inc.)

120

thoughts that come up unsolicited and at random, the result of all your hard work and experience. The benefit of this state is that you have an even better feel for what the market is "thinking" and so can pick better trades. You strengthen your intuitive decision making by not questioning it, and by moving full speed ahead without looking back once you make an intuitive trading decision. Again, you can do this comfortably, confidently, and competently only after you have done your left-brain homework thoroughly.

No, it's not easy to do all the work necessary to gain the hardcore left-brain experience in trading. It takes time, effort, work, energy, and money. It's not easy to do the work of knowing yourself and becoming fully conscious. Nor is it easy to be comfortable being alone, physically, emotionally, or in your decision making. But all these steps are necessary to become the best trader and maximize *The Art of the Trade.*

MANAGING INFORMATION

You know there are endless amounts of information available. The Internet has made this abundantly clear. And you will never know everything perfectly. You would quickly run out of time, money, and energy in the pursuit of infinite information. You reach the point in time when further input is no longer possible. You have to take action and make a decision. The better your gut instinct—your intuitive decision making—the better you will be able to process the reality of the imperfection of life, and implement *The Art of the Trade.*

You will be more willing to make mistakes, because you know you will not stumble for long. You will see yourself as always growing, learning, changing, doing the hard work analytically with the left brain and making more and more decisions to build up trust in your intuitive decision-making capabilities, stemming from the right brain. In the 1970s, a client of mine, excellent NBA free-throw shooter Mike Newlin, then a guard for the Houston Rockets, was asked during an interview why he was so good. He answered that he never thought about himself or what would happen if he were to miss a free throw. He never worried what the coach, his teammates, or the fans would think. He just focused on the mechanics, on what it took to shoot a free throw accurately. He relaxed and intuitively did what he knew how to do. That gave him the confidence to shoot a successful free throw.

KNOWING WHAT AND HOW TO CHANGE

You need to allow yourself time to freewheel, to do things like exercising so the intuitive can come to the surface. The intuitive will bring together the sense of the big picture necessary for the best trading decisions. You need to make sure that you have quiet time so that "still, small voice" can communicate to you. You will then frolic in childlike spontaneity.

Of course, all the above may require some change. If you want anything to change, you have to begin by changing yourself. You need to assess the situation rather than judge it. You have to establish a new belief system that will in turn alter the way you subjectively perceive reality, think about reality, and emotionally respond to it. Then your behavior will change.

There is a tremendous market for self-help products and services (the *New York Times* bestseller list even has a separate section for advice and how-to books). Many people attend self-improvement seminars and leave feeling committed to changing all aspects of their lives, only to return home and watch their best intentions fade into the frenzy of their harried routine. How can you really effect change in yourself? For starters, you must realize this is a journey of 1000 miles that begins with the first step. You must schedule what activities you will change, put them in your day timer, and write in future dates of your diary, so you can look back and see how well you've implemented your planned changes. Remind yourself all the time of your priority to make a change.

You can also ask someone to work with you, someone whom you can talk with and relate to about your trading activity, to prompt you or ask you periodically how you're doing on the par-

ticular area you want to change. This gives you some built-in
support and discipline to keep you on track, much as the lines
on the road keep you driving in the correct lane and the signs remind you of the speed limit. Again, a change in behavior often
requires a change in belief and in the value system that allows
you, subjectively, to perceive the world differently. When you
think and respond emotionally in a different fashion, you in turn
behave differently. It's a matter of spiritual, intellectual, emotional, and behavioral integration.

The final result is ultimately a change of behavior. You will
know what your intention is and will be attentive to it as the al-
tered behavior is manifested. You will receive signals and information in a humble, nonjudgmental way and look for the essence of the truth, regardless of what it may be. Finally, you will
surrender to that truth and respond mentally, emotionally, and
behaviorally in appropriate fashion.

You also need to learn to recognize and accept what you cannot
change. For instance, in my early years of trading, it used to bug
me that the local traders in some thin, low-volume markets, such
as pork bellies, would run the protective stops because they knew
where they were placed. Then they'd turn the market around and
take it the other way. I felt like this was thievery and piracy. It vio-
lated my sense of what is right, fair, and just. For example, just this
summer, prior to a holiday weekend, the local traders ran up August pork bellies to above 60 cents by bidding prices higher (see
Figure 7.3). There were not enough sell orders at normal resistance because no one was there trading—there was next to no liquidity. So traders with protective stops were vulnerable to locals
running prices up through thin resistance to pick off their stops.
The locals can tell where the resistance is, where a cluster of protective stops will be (just on the other side of resistance), and then
trigger these stops sitting in the market and force traders on the
short side to buy back their positions. The next six trading sessions,
pork bellies fell to 50 cents. Traders who were on the short side
would have been correct, if the locals had not run the protective
stops before prices collapsed.

It took several years before I realized that I could feel vio-
lated if I wanted to, but that it would do me harm and I couldn't

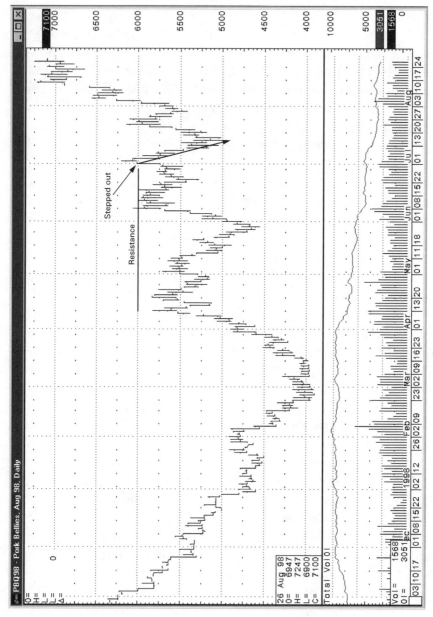

FIGURE 7.3 August 1998 pork bellies (Copyright 1998 CQG, Inc.)

change the situation. It's just part of the market. The only person I was really hurting was myself, by allowing the situation to draw down my psychological capital and by losing my focus on trades and opportunities in front of me. What I could change was my response. I was best served by staying relaxed. A lot of traders get hung up there. They get anxious and try, dangerously, to second-guess what's going on. The key is to stick with your own protective stop loss and be comfortable regardless of the result. Unless you're a day trader who is on top of the market, you are unlikely to profit in this situation. It's not something I would try to do. But even day traders, unless they are actually on the trading floor, cannot execute their trades as quickly as the local traders, and they don't have the extra input (feel) that the locals have by being in the pit. My advice: Accept an unpleasant trading situation, walk away, and look for other trading opportunities that have better possibilities.

Most people would rather die than change. All of us struggle to perceive reality accurately. We all see reality subjectively, according to how we were programmed. It is painful, hard work to change our internal programming to perceive reality accurately. The markets are blatant reality. They are what they are. We have to deal with how our own issues, with which we have been programmed, color the way we perceive the markets. When trading, we are forced to interface with an objective market. The clash between this stark reality and our subjective perception brings up our unresolved issues: how we subconsciously feel about ourselves, how much money we feel we deserve to make, whether we self-destruct. The markets will root out all this. We distort market reality with our issues. Resolving those issues is just as important as having a successful trading and money management system. In fact, we very well may not be able to trade successfully long term until we resolve these issues.

WATCHING YOUR LANGUAGE

Words are powerful. Monitoring your language will help you stay in the present, in the now. If you find yourself using such phrases as "I'm fearful," "I'm worried," and "I'm anxious," you'll know that you're living in the future and that you're also unconscious in the present. Your thoughts, and the way you express those thoughts, tend to be a self-fulfilling prophecy. Negative thoughts can usher in negative experiences. Positive thoughts attract positive outcomes. Scott Adams, creator of the Dilbert comic strip, offers a poignant example of the power of words in *Newsweek's* August 12, 1996, issue. Adams, who majored in economics and spent years buried in cubicle 4S700R at Pacific Bell's headquarters in northern California, recalls: "I figured that if you worked hard and you were smart you could get promoted. It wasn't until I was well into it when I realized that you also had to be tall and have good hair." He found much of his work meaningless, although his experiences with incompetent and egotistical bosses and petty corporate politics provided plenty of material for his satire of the American workplace. Adams attributes his eventual fortune and fame to positive affirmations. "The basic idea," he told *Newsweek*, "is that 15 times a day, you just write down whatever it is your goal is. Then you'll observe things happening that will make that objective more likely to happen. It's actually a process of forcing your environment to change."

His initial attempt concerned winning the attention and affection of a certain woman, and of selecting stocks that would rise in price. Both wishes came true, so he decided to affirm that he would get the precise score of 94 on the business school entrance exam he was about to take. He scored 94. Adams' next attempt was to write "I will become a syndicated cartoonist" 15 times a day. He packaged some doodles of a Dilbert-like character and sent them off to several syndicators. Sure enough, there was one acceptance letter amid the pile of rejections. So he upped the ante and began writing "I will be the best cartoonist on the planet." He also started willing the two main competitors in the field—the Far Side's Gary Larson and Calvin and Hobbes creator Bill Waterson—to retire, and they did. The rest is history. Today you can be sure Scott Adams is not looking back, but ahead.

You have to understand that the present rides one wing on the past and the other wing on the future. You learn from the past and you plan for the future. But the only time you get to act, the only time you are conscious and alive, is in the present, in the now. You can best respond to the information of the market by recognizing that there's no Holy Grail, no perfect system. There are just opportunities to respond. The present may have some similarities to the past in the market, but there will always be differences. Being present allows you to spot these differences and thereby make savvier trades.

KNOWING WHO YOU ARE

Don't get me wrong. It is better for long-term traders to use a left-brain technical trading system (e.g., moving averages) that keeps them in harmony with their psychological profile. If you are a swing trader, it is important to use relative strength indicators and stochastic indicators to trade the swings in the market. Everything must be harmonized with who you really are. You need to develop a comprehensive trading system that is consistent with the real you. It is difficult to consistently trade someone else's system successfully—unless, of course, you are very much like that other person. As discussed in detail in Chapter 5, you have to find a system that works for you. For that to happen, you have to know who you are and act accordingly.

When you can see yourself more objectively and match that reality to a compatible trading system, you can really give yourself over to it and bring more discipline to your trading. At the same time, you will bring more energy to trading and to more fully becoming what you give yourself permission to be. This was the lesson that Will had to learn in the 1998 award-winning movie *Good Will Hunting*.

In trading, we are always attempting to understand the future, the unknown, the uncertain. In a sense, this is spiritual, yin, magnetoelectric. Unless you have the capability to operate in that realm, you will limit your success or simply be mechanical. You will not, however, be in harmony with *The Art of the Trade*. Such is a place of total balance. This is not easy to achieve in the high-stress, fast-paced, cynical arena of trading.

The Art of the Trade really does require you to be different from nearly everyone else. It means you may need to live in a remote, quiet environment in order to trade successfully. You do need quiet time. Outer environmental peace may be necessary for internal peace to flourish. It may help you be more in touch with your own uniqueness. The more you know who you are—your strengths and weaknesses—and the more you are consistent with who you are, the better you will be able to deal with the markets and trading.

Although you need to find some quiet space of your own, you also need to surround yourself with people who are kind and supportive of the real you. Certainly, environmental tranquility and inner personal harmony are supportive of your internal peace of mind so that you can be more focused on your trading, more objective, and not get too close to the markets.

The best professional traders strive for the attitude that they're not emotionally attached to the outcome of their trades, but see them all as growing and learning experiences. Then regardless of what happens, the traders stay unperturbed. They know that they win regardless of the outcome of the trade, because they learn from their losses and gains. They learn how to better respond to losses and better appreciate wins, thereby stacking the odds in their favor to have more successful future trades. They have no expectations of the trade; they just do the best they can and let the results take care of themselves.

LETTING GO OF CONTROL, APPROVAL, AND SECURITY

Again, making money is a by-product of doing things correctly. Michael Jordan certainly doesn't think about how much money he's going to make in a particular NBA game when he goes out on the basketball court. Instead, he thinks about playing the game professionally, the best he can, because he loves it. Then the money he makes takes care of itself. Trading the markets requires exactly the same mentality. The by-product of doing things correctly is making money.

So you have to let go of the need for control, approval, and security. Some people believe they can control most everything in life. This a myth. Ironically, many of those who trade have a great need for control. But look at the evidence on how little control they truly have. Your autonomic nervous system and your subconscious control up to 90 percent of your body functions and behavior. So you may control 10 percent of portions of your own body at best.

When we were children, we had major control, security, and approval issues. Children crave the approval of their parents. A very controlling, insecure, and fearful parent, particularly when it comes to money, will affect the development of the child. In close personal relationships and in financial matters, the child, seeking approval, will tend to be like the parent. Parents provide security and control for their children. As we mature, we need to learn to be more responsible for ourselves, exercising self-control, realizing that life is insecure and risky, and that approval of others depends (hopefully) on how well we serve them. Moreover, as adults, we need to resolve the remnants of the four main psychological issues that affected us as children: fear of rejection, abandonment, chaos in life, and loud noises. These issues are brought to us early in life.

Traders who deal with these issues before they approach the market should be able to trade more successfully. They have less baggage. All traders must confront the way they approach family, love, sex, and money, how they deal with their parents, how they respond to authority and boundaries, and how they express basic emotions such as sad, mad, glad, and scared. These are all inner-core issues, and they begin to shape us in the womb, starting with the need for control, approval, and security.

You cannot control the weather, much of the food that you eat and drink when you're traveling, or how the other driver comes down the opposite lane of a two-lane road toward you. You don't control electricity or the weather or the government for the most part. The fact is, you control very little in life, so you might as well give up the attempt to control everything, do what you can responsibly, and leave the rest in God's hands. When you give up the myth of control you let go of the myth of the associated stress that comes from your futile attempts at control. It moves you into a better place where you can relax, be content, do the best you can, and operate in a trading methodology at a higher level.

You have already seen that the need for approval and the tendency to go along with the crowd loses money long term and violates the principle of *The Art of the Trade*. You have to be willing to stand alone, to operate according to the principle of contrary opinion. Few men and women will walk this exalted path mentally and emotionally, as discussed in the key points of this chapter. You have to run the risk of being seen as a kook, an oddball. But you will probably be somewhat of a kook if you are independently successful at trading. You have to give up your need for approval.

Finally, you have to give up your need for security. Security is a myth in this risk-filled, short life. I reflect on the situation in my poetry book *A Highlander's Passion* (Mountain Spring Press, 1997). The title of the poem, "Bull's-Eye," underscores how little security there really is, how life challenges you to give up your womb-based needs.

BULL'S-EYE

We enter this world alone, uncomfortably, out of control, with nothing,
facing the unknown.
We depart this world alone, uncomfortably, out of control, with nothing,
facing the unknown.
In between, we spend our lives (for the most part) avoiding being alone and
uncomfortable, controlling,
Striving to accumulate something, fleeing the unknown.
Why?
It's foolishness.
We flee the inevitable.
The finish is like the start.
Besides, in between we know not how much time we have.

Life's key then is to be settled, relaxed, at peace with being alone, uncomfortable,

not in control, with nothing, and the unknown.
All else is a futile escape from reality, a self-styled delusion,
a cruel joke we play on ourselves, self-deception.
We are frantically busy unconsciously chasing our own tails.
We can never return to the known security of our mother's womb
where we were never alone, were comfortable, controlled, and
wanted for nothing.
The full illumination of this folly stops us dead in our tracks.
Then we can at last be still, alive, and know God.
We can more fully appreciate good company, comfort, order, the
trappings of life and
knowing.
We can be human BEINGS instead of human DOINGS.

How then shall we live in this precious, precarious, short middle?
Consciously, compassionately, considerately, caringly, lovingly,
faithfully, responsibly,
humbly.
When we face the truth of the beginning and the end,
we can more wisely live the middle.
We can live truly free, discarding our invisible chains.

For what unique and higher purpose have we been created and
called?
When we discover and develop that plumb line, that living laser
beam, and abide in it,
we have enveloped the essence of life.
We have escaped the snare of self-deception.

By becoming content with whatever the market brings your
way, by being unattached to the outcome, with no expectations,
you are better able to give up the myth that perfectionism is possible in the market. You are far better off, instead, living by
Pareto's law of optimization: the 80/20 rule. By optimizing your
trading, you increase your choices in trading and in life. You can
achieve excellence and can be satisfied with excellence, even
though excellence is not perfection. The cost of perfection is too
high and, in fact, is unachievable. You cannot control the market, so the market will inevitably disappoint you; therefore, your
trading will always be an imperfect art. Focusing on attempting

to trade perfectly often keeps you dwelling on your past mistakes and fearful or hesitant regarding the future.

Again, the goal is excellence, not perfection. Perfectionism robs you of your health and takes an inordinate and unreasonable amount of time, money, and effort to hope (falsely) to achieve. Perfectionism leaves you unbalanced in life. You can optimize your trades by seeing trades as buses. A new one and a good one, although not a perfect one, comes along every 15 minutes or so. It's better to miss a bus (or a trade) than to run in the rain unsuccessfully for two and a half miles attempting to catch the one that you missed. Nor are you served by sitting at the bus stop worrying about the bus (or trade) that you missed while two more pass you by.

You can control when you enter and exit a trade. You can control your risk with money management. You can control whatever systems you use to trade the market. You can control your mental and emotional processes and behavior. But you cannot control the market. Therefore, you will never feel secure when it comes to the market. Nor will the market ever give you its approval. It could not care less. You have to jettison the womb-based needs of control, approval, and security if you are to become the best trader you can possibly be. You will find, instead, where your cross hairs of motivation and aptitude intersect and operate from that point. If you're motivated to trade with a particular trading system but don't have the aptitude for it, then you will work hard with at best mediocre success, or maybe even fail. Intuition is unlikely to kick in. If you have the aptitude to understand a trading system that is highly technical, both mathematically and scientifically, but aren't motivated to use it, you will squander your talents, probably be merely mediocre, and likely fail. You have to find out what suits you and who you really are to do well and be content. Pull together a trading system that you're motivated to work with and have the aptitude for. Then you can more likely trade successfully.

There is a balance between doing—working, trading, making money—and being—standing still, knowing, having that downtime, that quiet time. If you are going to make money long term in the markets and do well, you have to have time to "be,"

THE MENTALITY OF THE TRADE   **133**

to let your psychological reserves rebuild, to let your intuition percolate up insight. But you need first to learn, to grow, to read books, to attend seminars, to "do." It is important to continue to learn and grow. Jack D. Schwager is an old friend of mine. I have learned a great deal from his books published by Harperbusiness, *Market Wizards,* August 1989, and *The New Market Wizards,* August 1995. Robert Koppel and Howard Abell's *The Inner Game of Trading: Creating the Winner's State of Mind* (Irwin Professional Publishing, 1997) has been equally helpful. Koppel and Abell discuss the four C's of trading: commitment, conviction, constructing new patterns of behavior, and conditioning. Notice the similarity with what you've read herein. Truth has a funny way of crossing over.

Warning: Don't just read books about technical trading techniques and the new methodologies for making a million dollars in the next 24 hours. Balance technical reading with books and articles on the psychological arena. Remember, you are both a spiritual being and a physical being. These two aspects of your needs for both love and money have to be maintained and balanced. Psychological and financial capital are recognition of these two basic essences: your spiritual and material nature. When you keep these two in balance long term, you survive and prosper, and remain a lot happier. Moreover, you move into the arena of *The Art of the Trade.*

A large number of successful traders and investors subscribe to newsletters. They can give you a unique perspective plus insight and clues into the trading markets. They can also bring reinforcement about what you're doing that helps you better prepare, both psychologically and financially, your own investment trading program.

There's an old saying, "The greatest bargain available is the low cost of good advice." Why has this been true century after century? Because very few people are willing to learn the easy way, which is from the experience and wisdom of others, from good advice. Most folks would rather learn from their own mistakes, which is the hard way to learn.

I have found that those who are wise and prudent are those who are continually reading, learning, and growing. They are normally the most successful. They are also the ones to whom other people go for advice and counsel when it hurts less to change than to stay stuck in unproductive present behavior. Don't discount the importance of mental, spiritual, and emotional growth, left-brain and right-brain integration, leading to financial and psychological development.

THE EMOTIONS OF THE TRADE

As discussed in Chapter 6, there is a mentality to trading—thought processes—that affects trading and is affected by trading. Similarly, all sorts of emotions impact how you trade, just as a spectrum of emotions can be triggered by trading. Your emotions can work with you and enhance your trading, or they can work against you and cloud your objectivity, erode your patience, and tempt you to make rash decisions that violate your trading system and money management plan. This chapter will help you better understand and manage your emotions, which in turn will improve your ability to trade successfully, to handle losses, and to appreciate wins.

Emotion blocks accurate perception. A thought moves through the emotional center of the brain before it is processed in the logic center. To minimize the emotional charge, you must see trading as a business (as discussed in Chapter 4). Losses are simply a part of the cost of doing business. When a sales rep makes x number of sales calls, he or she will have y number of sales, or wins, and z number of no-sales, or losses. Both sales calls and trading involve the investment of time and money. You must learn what you can from your experiences. The more you learn, the more you know where and when to make sales calls, and the better you will know when and where to trade. Simultaneously, you must see trading as a game, and learn how to play the game correctly. Making money is a by-product of doing things (trading) correctly, of playing the game right. Emotion can get in the way of competent execution.

HARNESSING SPIRITUALITY AND SCIENCE

This means, of course, that you need to live more spiritually than materially. What does trading have to do with spiritual matters? Isn't trading based on money, the essence of materialism itself? Yes, trading involves money and is by and large a means of increasing money. However, as pointed out in Chapter 2, a trader who trades with only the money in mind, who is not in tune with creation, nature, and the spiritual life, will be unlikely to maintain a healthy emotional attitude about, and approach to, trading.

Philip S. Callahan, a philosopher and scientist, has observed the intricate ways of people and nature. His breakthrough discoveries about how insects communicate have led to numerous improvements in agriculture and aerospace. In his book *Tuning In to Nature: Solar Energy, Infrared Radiation, and the Insect Communication System* (Devin-Adair, 1975), Callahan reveals his theory of reverse bionics—the study of technology as a guide to understanding nature (as opposed to bionics, which is the study of nature as a way of understanding and improving technology).

After studying electronics in the U.S. Air Force, Callahan returned to his original passion of biology (specifically, the study of insects). As he was studying the corn earworm moth, a destructive agricultural pest, he noticed that

> the shapes and forms of electronic antennas that I had so diligently struggled to erect on the air fields of Europe and Asia suddenly appeared before me as drawings in the early literature of insect antennae. . . . I recognized that the sensilla (spine) structure, which has evolved over millions of years on insect antennae, resembles to a startling degree—and in miniature—what man had already designed to catch frequencies that he was hurling about the globe in the microwave region of the spectrum.

Other scientists have noticed, too, how reverse bionics operates. Carl Feit, a cancer biologist at Yeshiva University in New York and a Talmudic scholar, finds evidence that "something about human consciousness is harmonious with the mind of God." As Feit explained in *Newsweek*'s July 20, 1998, cover story, "Science Finds God," "Humans invent abstract mathematics, basically making it up out of their imaginations, yet math magically turns out to describe the world. Greek mathematicians divided the circumference of a circle by its diameter, for example, and got the number pi, 3.14159. ... Pi turns up in equations that describe subatomic particles, light, and other quantities that have no obvious connections to circles." John Polkinghorne, a distinguished physicist at Cambridge University before he became an Anglican priest in 1982, told *Newsweek* that "our minds, which invent mathematics, conform to the reality of the cosmos. We are somehow tuned in to its truths."

To the extent that we are tuned into the spiritual truths underpinning science and mathematics, we can better understand the way we, as part of creation, work. The key for traders is to apply reverse bionics to the markets: to find lessons in science, technology, and religion that mirror the human-made markets. Such an understanding can improve performance in trading.

One of the best examples of how creation applies to the market is the effectiveness of the Fibonacci ratio (also called the golden mean), which is approximately 0.618, and its inverse, 1.618. The ratio is derived by dividing any two successive numbers in the Fibonacci sequence, in which each number equals the sum of the preceding two numbers (0, 1, 1, 2, 3, 5, 8, 13, 21, 34, etc.). For example, $0 + 1 = 1$; $1 + 1 = 2$; $1 + 2 = 3$, $2 + 3 = 5$. The ratio of any two consecutive numbers equals the Fibonacci ratio (for example, $13 \div 21 = 0.618$, or about 62 percent).

Throughout nature (sunflowers, pineapples, grapefruits, shells, and pussy willows), art (DaVinci, Seurat, and Mondrian), and architecture (the Parthenon and Egyptian pyramids), you will find the Fibonacci ratio at work. For instance, the number of petals that spiral up a pine cone is almost always a Fibonacci number. I have done bar chart analysis of the way mountain ranges peak and trough. I have calculated that a dip in one mountain was a 38 percent correction, in another a 62 percent correction, and so on. That's Fibonacci.

Robert Prechter's Elliott wave theory is based on the Fibonacci ratio. Here's how Elliott Wave International's Web site (www. elliottwave.com) describes the connection between the two:

> One of Elliott's most significant discoveries is that because markets unfold in sequences of five and three waves, the number of waves that exist in the stock market's patterns reflects the Fibonacci sequence of numbers (0, 1, 1, 2, 3, 5, 8, 13, 21, 34, etc.), an additive sequence that nature employs in many processes of growth and decay, expansion and contraction, progress and regress. Because this sequence is governed by the ratio, it appears throughout the price and time structure of the stock market, apparently governing its progress.
>
> What the Wave Principle says, then, is that mankind's progress (of which the stock market is a popularly determined valuation) does not occur in a straight line, does not occur randomly, and does not occur cyclically. Rather, progress takes place in a "three steps forward, two steps back" fashion, a form that nature prefers. As a corollary, the Wave Principle reveals that periods of setback in fact are a requisite for social (and perhaps even individual) progress.

Markets are always seeking balance, or equilibrium: between bulls and bears, longs and shorts. When a market moves up, it will then often seek to retrace its move with a 50 percent correction. Or, when a market moves down, it will often look to rally by 50 percent. There tends to be a natural overshoot or undershoot, which just seems to be part of human nature, toward too little or excess. So it's not unusual for a market to correct 38 percent or 62 percent, which is 12 percent on either side of 50 percent. Hello Fibonacci!

A technical tool called speed resistance lines is based on one-third and two-thirds retracement of a price move from high to low, or from low to high. I think these lines work better with the more precise Fibonacci ratios of 0.382 and 0.618. I use them as a way of looking for the price at which a market will stop correcting, whether it's support or resistance. In addition, Fibonacci ratios can be applied to swing moves from lows to highs or from highs to lows. Often the next move will be either 38 percent of the previous move or 62 percent or 1.62 percent of the previous swing move. The result gives you price targets for the next move up or down, as the case may be.

However, you should realize that as Callahan warned in *Tuning In to Nature,* "the fact that one utilizes the scientific method—by definition an objective method—does not confer immunity to the passions and fervor leading to wrong conclusions."

If you have too big of a hangup with regard to money, greed, winning, ego, or being right, you will never be the best trader you can be. If you stay relaxed, with a sense of humor, you will develop in this crucial area where trading becomes a skillful art. You will recognize your mistakes and errors more quickly in trading. You'll learn when to trust and not trust others, as well as information that comes to you. You'll be more forgiving of yourself when you make a mistake. You will better understand other people, including the players in the market, so you can better understand the trades that you are about to enter or have entered. In short, you will become a more objective trader, in touch with market reality.

FINE-TUNING THE EMOTIONAL WAVES WE BROADCAST

One of the insights resulting from studies of the intensity of emotion and the electromagnetism of the human body is that the human body measures intensity. Philip Callahan illustrates the importance of the electromagnetic spectrum—which he calls the "unsensed environment"—in *Tuning In to Nature:* "A basic understanding of the electromagnetic spectrum is central to any understanding of our environment. We all live in a world of radiation, only a small part of which is visible." Figure 8-1 shows the electromagnetic spectrum between radio and ultraviolet in terms of wavelengths, as measured in micrometers (one-thousandth of a millimeter). As Callahan explains:

> All frequencies shorter than 1 meter long (100 centimeters) down to 1 millimeter long are called microwave

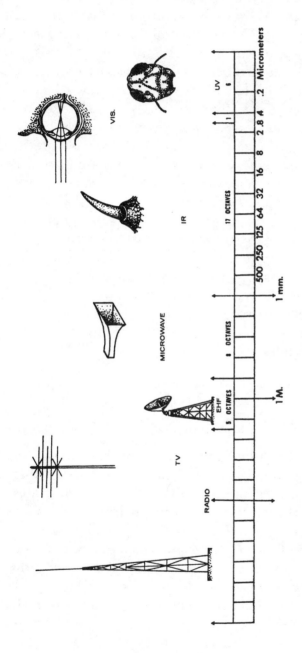

FIGURE 8.1   The electromagnetic spectrum

Source: *Tuning In To Nature: Solar Energy, Infrared Radiation, and the Insect Communication System*, by Philip S. Callahan (The Devin-Adair Company, 1975).

frequencies. High-resolution radar and guidance systems operate in this region. From 1 millimeter down to 0.7 micrometers (red), where human eyes see, is the infrared portion of the spectrum. This almost unexplored region of the spectrum contains 17 octaves of radiation and is the largest region. It is also in the natural "sea" of radiation where we dwell day and night on this spaceship Earth. Human beings cannot see beyond 0.4 micrometers (violet), but insects see into the ultraviolet to slightly below 0.36 micrometers.

You, as a living antenna, broadcast the intensity of whatever emotional charge you experience; you will tend to duplicate an emotionally intense experience over and over again until you no longer engage, become detached, dissipate its energy, and handle it calmly. So what you want to do is minimize emotional intensity, particularly the negative intensities, or else you'll attract them over and over again in your trading. This is the application of what Callahan is expressing scientifically. We cannot see (literally) what we are broadcasting.

That's why people tend to make the same mistakes over and over again. They never really learn. As long as they carry (broadcast) the same emotional charge (in the infrared range of the light spectrum), particularly with their mistakes, their bodies are saying, "We like this intensity, this high, even if it's a negative one." So they will continue to broadcast the frequency of this emotion and attract it back again and again.

One of my weaknesses in trading was that I would let some losses run because emotionally I had difficulty admitting when I was wrong. The market would reward me often enough for that error (of violating my discipline regarding protective stop losses and my money management system) that it served as a periodic reinforcement for this dangerous behavior. I would hang on to trading reverses past my protective stop loss because more times

---

The market finds every chink in your armor, every weakness, every character flaw, because you broadcast these traits, and then attract trades that challenge your imperfections.

than not it would work out—the market would come back in my favor, and I would get back to breakeven or even make a small profit. However, the danger was (and it occurred) that sooner or later a huge market price spike would move against me and take a chunk out of my capital. All it takes is one or two such major disasters, where you let your losses run, to wipe you out. Generally, under such circumstances, you have to be wrong only 20 percent of the time to be wiped out. This means you can be right 80 percent of the time and still experience huge net losses.

The thing was, I had a real emotional charge—based upon successful behavior in an earlier time in my life—invested in letting losses run and being right. Being right in any given trade was emotionally and unconsciously more important to me at the time than long-term profits and losses. It was tied to my very sense of survival. Until I was able to let go of the emotional charge of whether I was right or wrong in a trade, I was not able to control or exercise the discipline of good money management—cutting losses short. So the market kept bringing this same issue around to me time and time again, until I let go of the charge. The market finds every chink in your armor, every weakness, every character flaw.

In one of my poems, "Does It Ever Cross Your Mind?" I wrote: "What we resist we attract, what we need we combat." We have a natural tendency to move toward entropy, decay, and death. Children tend to eat food that tastes good even if it is not nutritious—like soft drinks, candy, and potato chips—instead of gravitating to natural, fresh, and alive foods, such as vegetables and fruit, which feed and support the body. Similarly, you broadcast negative traits and attract those trades that challenge your imperfections, much in the same way as you attract people in your life who will bring up your unresolved, emotionally charged relationship issues.

It took me about three years to overcome my emotionally charged challenge to be right. Consider that I had been trained as an instructor pilot in supersonic aircraft, where I'd be flying a jet (T-38) at .86 mach. If you're wrong in this situation, you're quite literally dead. Precise accuracy was required to stay alive! So to me, being right was tied to survival. I had to reverse this concept of being right in the market, where being wrong is attached to financial survival. Put differently, it is the willingness to be wrong and quickly admit it in trading the markets that is key to success and survival. This took a lot of reprogramming for me. It is a problem that engineers, doctors, and lawyers tend to have in their trading too. Their professional training programs them to be invested intellectually and emotionally in being right, precisely accurate. But holding on to the need to be right will punish you in the market. Being able to admit when you're wrong rewards you. This is not an easy program to reverse for many successful people in walks of life other than trading.

For me, the market would bring up the same issue over and over again, until I reached the point at which I no longer cared whether I was right. I just wanted to do the right thing. It wasn't until I relaxed and breathed through the emotional charge and was able to say, "I don't have to be right," that my trading changed permanently for the better. Then, whenever the market would bring the challenge to me, I'd handle it more correctly—I would cut any losses short. Once I was able to do that on a consistent basis, without the emotional charge of the need to be right, I was no longer attracted to trades where that emotional charge challenged me. I had learned my lesson.

Michael Ryce, a doctor of naturopathic medicine and holistic philosophy with a background in electronics and business, calls this broadcast of emotions a psychic megaphone. "Every reality in your mind sets up an energy wave to attract people who are in tune with that reality," he wrote in *Why Is This Happening to Me . . . Again?! . . . And What You Can Do About It!* (self-published, 1997). "The people we attract then trigger the reality within us, but the trigger does not cause our feelings, it only resonates what is already there." Ryce points out that Marcel Vogel, a former IBM research scientist, "was able to measure the high energy waves that leave the mind when we think a thought."

In this same vein, the biblical caution to "be anxious about nothing" (Philippians 4:6) is pivotal to successful trading. Regardless of what occurs in your trading, you must learn emotionally to take it in stride. You have to develop a relaxed mental attitude about everything, and not react to anything. Sure, this is difficult to do. Dealing with money is an emotionally charged issue for most traders. But when you're anxious about nothing, you are not giving off signals that attract trades that trigger the emotional charge that creates trading losses. Remember, "The Lord giveth, and the Lord taketh away, blessed be the name of the Lord." As with Job in the Old Testament, the challenge is to live in a joyful, thankful state, regardless of what your circumstances are, to have that internal peace that passes all understanding.

One of the ways I find myself best able to approximate this state of being is to view myself not as an owner of anything, which would tend to bring an attachment and an emotional charge, but as a steward of whatever money and material goods I have responsibility for. As a steward, I'm passing this way only for a short time. I have limited time and knowledge. I am imperfect. I will make mistakes. I can only do my best and then move forward. I look at the people who've lived throughout history, who had money and material goods much greater than my own, and wonder: In the big scheme of life, how important was their wealth? I'm no different than they were in terms of the mass ocean of humanity that has passed through time in linear history. How to handle appropriately what we have may be one of the most important lessons to learn while we're on this earth. I came in with nothing, I will leave with nothing. Seeing myself as a steward of what I acquire while I am on this earth puts me in a much more relaxed state of mind, with a lower emotional charge. It keeps me more balanced in weighing what is important in life. It makes me a better manager of assets, and a better trader. It causes me to be more objective.

That's not to say you should live your life devoid of emotion and passion. Quite the contrary. Your emotions are correctly the heart's responder to solid values and the head's grounded accurate thinking. So, then, emotions become a choice, with healthy boundaries that flow from a grounded base rather than being automatically, naturally reactive to stimuli. You can enjoy your emotions with greater appreciation, rather than experience them as a reaction to a random roller-coaster ride of circum-

stances over which you have no control. I'm not saying you should emulate Mr. Spock of *Star Trek* fame. Emotions are optimally like a manicured garden that can bring tremendous joy rather than a tumultuous, thorn-and-thistle-infested wilderness that tears your clothing and causes you to bleed unpredictably.

Nature and creation will test your character. Your emotional responses can become a choice rather than a reaction. When you choose how you will emotionally respond, that's a sign of discipline and maturity.

According to Bob Beutlich, an avant-garde scientist, the physical body operates at 1C (C equals the speed of light), and the mental body at 3C, but the emotional body oscillates at 2.5C, between the mental and physical body. So the emotional body is a crucial link to physical well-being as well as mental health. Equally important, what goes on inside us spiritually and mentally shapes the emotional response. As we believe, as we think, as we feel, what we do, what we eat, so we are.

Stanley Keleman, author of *Your Body Speaks Its Mind: The Bio-Energetic Way to Greater Emotional and Sexual Satisfaction* (Center Press, 1981), describes how the higher-level frequencies (the mental body) rule over and determine the lower-level frequencies (emotions and the physical body). So what we believe determines how we think, which determines how we feel, which molds our bodies. It is therefore important that we set up our theoretical models accurately, as we reprogram ourselves, because they will determine how we subjectively view the facts of reality. How we think in turn influences how we will emotionally respond and behave, which will ultimately shape or mold our human bodies.

Broad emotional swings—spikes, as I call them—set up an emotional charge that a person broadcasts over and over again. This feverish activity burns up the body's minerals and vitamins, particularly the stress-related B vitamins. This drawdown in physical reserves drains psychological reserves, because B vitamins are key to psychological reserves. This mind/emotion/body connection has gained increasing recognition among scientists of all kinds, particularly in the field of psychoneuroimmunology.

Your reserve energy, which is measurable, is like an afterburner in a jet engine, which provides extra thrust when it is activated. Or it's like a runner's second wind. Reducing extreme emotional swings enhances your reserves of psychological and physical capital, which in turn enables you to better handle a greater number of intense challenges. The more relaxed you are, the better your digestive system functions—the stomach, intestines, liver, gall bladder, spleen, and pancreas. And this enables you to better assimilate critical nutrients and put them to good use in your body. The more at peace and relaxed the body is, the more efficiently it will run. Everything we do, we do better when we are relaxed—think, sing, play the piano, ski, play golf, or trade the markets.

MINIMIZING EMOTIONAL EXHAUSTION, WORRY, AND FEAR

To minimize an emotional charge, it helps if you become adept at stepping outside yourself. As described in Chapter 6, practice seeing yourself as your own best adviser, particularly when you are feeling emotional stress or a drawdown of financial or psychological capital. In other words, let's say you've had a hard night for some reason—the children were sick and you were up with them most of the night. You arise and have your trading plan from the night before, you look at the trades and you know they're going to trigger, but you're tired. Your psychological capital is drawn down. In this situation, you need to work consciously to remove yourself, and see yourself as a consultant looking at the trader (you) sitting before your computer screen. Ask yourself, "What would I advise the trader to do in this situation in the market?" All of a sudden, you're a consultant. You're objective. You've put yourself in a professional position outside your emotional self, removing the subjective perspective of the flawed way you would otherwise have approached the market.

You can do the same thing if you are feeling fearful regarding a trade. What would you tell someone else to do, knowing what you know about this market? Would you recommend exe-

cuting or not executing the trade? If you can become objective by seeing yourself as a consultant or adviser to yourself, you help preserve your psychological capital and reduce the emotional whipsaws and stress that plague traders year in and year out. It helps you to be objective rather than subjective. This approach is particularly beneficial when you have a fear of a loss or a fear of being wrong.

What about worry? I've always considered worry to be the devil's prayer; it's a nonproductive use of time and energy. If you can't do anything about a situation, why worry? Let it go. If you can do something about a situation, do it. Worry is a needless waste of time, energy, and emotion (psychological capital). You want to work ultimately to minimize your emotional charge, desensitizing everything. You don't want to become euphoric over your wins or depressed over your losses. You want to avoid emotional high peaks as well as deep valleys; you want to be steady and even-tempered. Stress, wherever you find it, is a killer long term.

EXERCISING PERSONAL FORGIVENESS

To preserve psychological capital, it is important to exercise personal forgiveness. You don't want to be too hard on yourself. As Michael Ryce points out in *Why Is This Happening to Me . . . Again?!*:

> When a negative reality is triggered, it is an opportunity to learn *True Forgiveness*. When pain surfaces, if you are honest and in touch with yourself, you will own the upset and seize the opportunity to release that internal reality—to *Forgive!* Pain functions to inform us of our errors.
>
> False forgiveness is based on the belief that others are responsible for what we feel, and therefore it tends to reinforce that error. To forgive others, in this manner, for what happens in your mind leaves your pain intact and the opportunity to heal is lost. Making use of every opportunity to heal is an important decision you can make and that decision will immeasurably accelerate your process.

You live in an environment of uncertainty; you have limited time, energy, and money in life. Sometimes you can do everything right and still fail. Failure usually stems from ignorance, arrogance, and/or carelessness. Sometimes, though, there are unfortunate things that just happen. You have to be able to forgive yourself and move on, learn, and grow. Of course, you always want to forgive others. Carrying past baggage will not do you any good; you must learn from the mistakes of your past and then apply them positively and constructively in the future. We live in an unfinished, imperfect world; it's incomplete now and will be so when we depart.

As people get older, they either get bitter or they get better. All of us want to get better, to build and preserve psychological capital. We desire the "better" things in life to come back to us rather than the "bitter" things. We want to broadcast and receive life, not death.

MASTERY OF SELF

Mastery of self includes integrating many of the insights and techniques that we examined in previous chapters. We're not wealthy unless we're healthy. We're not clear-headed mentally or emotionally unless we're healthy. Exercise and diet are critical, not only for performing well in the market but also for preserving psychological capital. As little as a 10 percent drawdown in physical or psychological capital is sufficient to turn a winner into a breakeven trader, or even a loser; health affects judgment. So you want to keep up to speed physically.

When I was younger, I used to get indignant about situations that didn't go my way. I'd say I was pretty typical. I was physically healthy, but I believe that if I had not started processing the ideas I've shared with you throughout this book, I would be less healthy, less successful in my trading, and less content with my life in general. What turned me around was a combination of observations. My son's epileptic seizures put me in touch with all sorts of alternative medical resources and psychological and scientific material. I began to receive invitations to speak at agricultural and holistic medicine conferences, where I was exposed to top experts in many related fields. I now speak at 15 to 20 conferences a year, in such diverse areas as global science, philosophy, religion, psychotronics, agriculture, commodity trading, investments, international currencies, politics, and health. It has been like having a human Internet of resources and data well before such existed on the computer.

Eventually, the idea occurred to me that all this information related to me. That realization opened me up to making profound changes in my life. I am fortunate to have been exposed to the many holistic medical, psychological, religious, and scientific works that I have integrated into my life and my trading. In this book, I share the essence of what I have learned that is helpful from my exposure to these diverse worlds, my voracious reading, and my gift of seeing how information dovetails across disciplines.

DOING WHAT IT TAKES TO GET AND STAY HEALTHY

For instance, I found that psychologically, with supportive people, I am able to smile and laugh frequently. This is healthy. Also, I make sure to keep my exercise activity totally different from my trading activity. Doing so helps me preserve my psychological capital. My recreational (exercise) activity is outside, whether it's skiing, hunting, fishing, or riding bikes or horses. It's nonmental, physical (requiring movement), and nonstressful. By contrast, analyzing the markets on a computer is an inside activity. It's mental, it can be stressful, and it's sedentary. So, I'm working to maintain a balance.

My diet is equally important. I am what I eat, just as I am what I believe, think, feel, and do. Live food, which is low-fat, natural, and fresh, is vital.

There are two products I have come across, one called Earth Manna and the other Illumination, that have been very, very helpful in terms of my state-of-the-art nutrition.

Earth Manna is a culture of naturally occurring, soil-based organisms (SBOs) and 71 natural vital chemicals and bioactive minerals and enzymes, in a supportive substrate. Earth Manna International, based in Phoenix, Arizona (800-528-0559), explains that the SBOs in Earth Manna eliminate putrification, including tarlike leathering in the colon. SBOs act like little Pac-Mans, cleaning out debris and breaking down hydrocarbons, so food can be better broken down to its basic elements and assimilated easily by the body. The company also says SBOs stimulate the immune system to create an army of antibodies that can attack foreign viruses, bacteria, or parasite invaders. I first became excited about Earth Manna because it literally saved my oldest son's life when he was having uncontrollable epileptic seizures.

Illumination, a daily phytonutrient, provides extracts of more than 30 of the South American rain forest's most valued botanical treasures, which can help cleanse, detoxify, strengthen, and revitalize most organs and systems of the body. Its manufacturer, Rainforest Bio Energetics (800-835-0850), says Illumination leads to renewed health, vitality, and general well-being, while promoting peak performance in our everyday lives. After taking these products for several years as daily supplements, I have been told by my doctors that my physiological age is 15 years younger than my biological age. My blood samples are so healthy that they have fooled doctors into thinking I am a marathon runner and a vegetarian (I am neither). I strongly urge you to investigate both Earth Manna and Illumination. They are worth their weight in gold to me.

REPROGRAMMING BAD HABITS

Emotional processing, as discussed previously, is important. Ninety-eight percent of people live by habit, doing whatever they learned in their first 10 to 12 formative years, when the delta, theta, alpha, and lower beta regions of the brain were being programmed. If you can process the error out and reprogram yourself, you expand your options of behavior. That's part of what life is all about—being able to expand our options of responses, our options of action, breaking old, nonproductive habits and establishing new, healthy ones.

Have you ever traded and said, "This is the same thing I've done over and over again?" Michael Ryce, author of *Why Is This Happening to Me . . . Again?*, has also produced a series of audiotapes and videocassettes. Ryce's tapes explain why this has happened to all of us, why it is so difficult to change, and how to break the jinx or nonproductive pattern. Ryce offers approaches and tools that can transform unhealthy thought processes, habits, emotions, relationships, and lifestyles into healthy ones. He explains:

> It takes time to build the brain cells for significant change to take place. . . . Brain cells are the body's storage system for information and "building brain cells" refers not to building physical structure but to storing information for future recall. . . . Unraveling old patterns and teaching your mind new ways to function takes time. Beware the tendency of the mind to reject what is inconsistent with your current beliefs. I suggest that you set aside anything that does not fit your thinking and see how those pieces work as you "build" new information into brain cells.

Ryce examines from a psychological perspective what Callahan and others explore from a scientific perspective (see Chapter 8). With totally different methodologies and evidence, they come up with effectively the same conclusions about the challenge of breaking out of inappropriate, ineffective, subconscious programming from the first 6 to 12 years of life. The parallel indicates that they have gotten in touch with a primary truth—just as, when a number of indicators dovetail in a market, you have an enhanced signal.

Another emotional processing technique that works not only to improve your ability to trade but also to increase your response capability in life is the Sedona Method, created by the Sedona Institute in Arizona (602-553-3770). The program, which includes videos and numerous workbooks, shows you how to feel your emotional pain in the diaphragm. The theory is that any time you are not processing information correctly emotionally, you shut down your breathing. The emotion gets tied up in the diaphragm and the breath shortens. When this happens you should ask such questions as, "Could I let it go? Would I let it go? When?" When you finally say, "Now," and then breathe through the negative emotions, they will process—and you will be more able to let them go.

Whenever we avoid processing a negative emotion, then attach an emotional charge to it, and shorten our breath and tighten our diaphragm, our blood pressure often shoots up so that we lock the memory of that emotional charge into our system. This is what happened to me back in July 1998 when my pork belly trade got stopped out on a thinly traded day by locals who were running up the price and gunning for the protective stops. If I am willing to accept the market for what it is, and that I can't do anything about what the market does, then I will neutralize the negative charge. That's the healthiest way to handle such situations. But if I let the issue dig into my sense of justice—how the local traders are taking unfair advantage of the traders in the market—I could feel I was robbed. I could have gotten angry, chewed out my broker, written to the exchange, and hollered—all with no positive outcome. The only result would have been my own negative emotional reaction—shortened breath, tightened diaphragm, and locked-in anger inside me. The Bible in Ephesians 4:26 says, "Don't let the sun go down on your wrath." When you go to sleep, the current in you literally reverses and you lock your daily emotional charges into your organ systems, body processes, and memory. It's a very negative thing to do. It ensures that you will have other challenges, that you'll be broadcasting those signals to attract similar trading situations. Processing the situation correctly short-circuits the negative cycle. So, before I go to sleep at night, I forgive others whom I think have wronged me and give thanks personally for all things. I want to stay free, healthy, and unencumbered.

I've worked on the Sedona Method for several years. I find when I start processing activities that repeat over and over again, whether it's trades in the markets that have gone awry or disputes with those close to me that have been repeated, my mentality starts to change as I process, and I see new ways of responding to the recurring situation. My thinking is no longer robotic or habitual. It becomes new and creative. Remember, emotions are a choice. The realm of unconscious bad habits is where the demons live in all of us. We need to exorcize them.

For the most part, you want to live in the present. You want to live in the "now" by mastery of self. This moment is really all you have. This moment is life! If you're going to be fully conscious and able to respond optimally, which is being responseable, you have to live in the present. The past is history, the future does not yet exist. You can act only in the here and now: not in the past, not in the future.

WHAT IT ALL MEANS FOR TRADERS

Let me put this in the frame of reference of the marketplace. Say you see an opportunity to trade the short side of stocks, but your heart and mind are still on that silver loss you took yesterday. You just can't quite let the frustration go. As a result, you're not able to focus on the stock trade. Has this ever happened to you? It's happened to me. It happens to a lot of us. It will help if you can keep your focus in the present, in the now, by telling yourself, "This is the moment. I've already learned what I can from the past. That's dead and gone. What I do now is going to affect what's going to happen in the future." These affirmations allow you to maintain your full level of consciousness, so you can respond objectively. You will make better judgments and decisions. As a result, not only will you preserve your psychological capital, but you will have the enhanced capacity to increase your financial capital in your trading.

Living in the present, jettisoning past baggage—false hope, fear of loss, fear of being wrong, shame, pride of opinion, guilt, wanting to be right—letting all that go and living in the now, being fully conscious and therefore fully able to respond, this is being alive! Being alive releases more incapacitating factors than anyone can ever imagine.

To sum up, the whole concept of being rich in psychological capital requires continually living consciously, in the present, being quiet, calm, personally balanced, centered, grounded, and aware, and living as much as possible in the area of certainty. These techniques are not theoretical. They are real. They increase financial capital and enhance its preservation.

I traded my first futures contracts and bought my first shares of stock when I was flying jets in the U.S. Air Force in the 1970s. I've been involved in these markets a long, long time. All the concepts, all the procedures and methodologies I've given you here, I've learned in more than 25 years of trading these markets. They are, to my mind, *The Art of the Trade*. They've all stood the test of time. I wouldn't share them with you unless I knew you could benefit from them and help fulfill your personal destiny.

Many of us have children whom we care about and love. We want the best for them. We want to prepare them for the challenges of life. I wrote the following three poems to help guide my children through the minefield of life. To me, they are just as valuable to a trader who wants to be successful in *The Art of the Trade*. In many ways, the poems summarize the insights presented in this book. I hope you find them useful.

TAKE HEED

Take heed, my child
For if they always praise you
One day they'll pull their knives
To cut and slash and slay you.

If they speak honeyed words
And tend to condescend
Don't believe what they say
Their hearts are a cold wind.

Never ever let yourself
Be put up on a pedestal
The tide can quickly turn
And you'll end up The Great Infidel.

You've often heard it said,
"Don't judge a book by its cover,"
For what appears attractive
May not love you like your father.

Do always beware
Of those who look so good

For when it comes to substance
Often they're decayed wormwood.

If they draw their strength
From fluff and stuff about them
Be assured no light's within
That can radiate from inside out of them.

If they only want to borrow
And never care to lend
Then you'll know when trouble comes
On them you must not depend.

Life is full of selfish takers
Few are those who love and give
Takers are miserable and dying
Givers have joy and light to live.

Take care and watch with whom
Folks spend their days, time, and money
This will tell you who they are
If they're to be trusted or if they're cunning.

Steer clear of those obsessed
Who must at all cost win
For ruthless competition
Is a deadly sin.

Avoid like the proverbial plague
Those ruled by just their feelings
They justify anything in their dark hearts
Leaving your heart bruised and reeling.

Instead use truth to guide your mind
As you choose your life's way
Then let your heart soften your path
As compassion leads day by day.

Cling to mentors with a vision
Those who have a long-term view
Making principled decisions
They know what's right to do.

True fortunes don't come easy
All that glitters is not gold
Hard work and service are what last
Wise men have long told us so.

Carefully choose your calling and your mate
These two decisions will mold your life's fate
It's not even a subject open to debate
Choosing either badly is a disastrous mistake.

Pick work for which you're suited
Matching motivation and aptitude
Such will bring you re-creation
Work that's drudgery makes you brood.

Pick a partner for your lifetime
With like interests, values, and flow
Supporting and balancing each other
Is worth more than you'll ever know.

Observe, too, carefully
Who you call your true friend
Mirroring each other
You two should stand through thick and thin.

Link up with those who cooperate
Who have abiding peace and quiet
Their friendship's good as gold
For no price could you buy it.

If in your gut you feel a knot
And your breath begins to shorten
Pay notice to these clues
For there may be something rotten.

Life will give you subtle signals
And if you'll only pay attention
Such will keep you out of trouble
Out of love all this I mention.

And if you always put God first
Do what's good, honorable, and just

Sunlight will follow your shadows
As spiritual gold is spun from dust.

WINNING IN LIFE

You say you want to win in life
Accomplish all of which you're capable
Then get up off your procrastinating duff
Take action, be responsible.

Decide clearly and precisely
Exactly what you want to do
Then with persistent perseverance
Work hard to see it through.

Don't be distracted by urgent stuff
Focus on what's important
Make plans progress toward your goal
Then to creativity's voice you shall harken.

Next, build a team of kindred souls
Who share your heart's desire
Working together, all with a stake
Fans the passion for your fire.

Look to serve before you're served
Make everyone a winner
The whole is greater than its parts
The pie gets bigger, not thinner.

Listen closely to what others say
Be humble and empathetic
Holding your tongue while others talk
Reaps dividends that are more than cosmetic.

Last, neglect not care of yourself
If you do, others also will
Growth, love, diet, exercise, and rest
Such sharpens all your skills.

OUR LIVES' FOUR SEASONS

The first season
We are like seeds
Thrust into the dark, warm earth.
We have no energy or life of our own.
We are programmed
The product of our genetics,
Our heredity, and our environment.
We have no choice concerning our ancestors.
We do not pick our parents.
Nor do we choose where,
Or the conditions under which,
We are raised.
For nearly all of us
What happens in these first two,
Three, six, and even twelve years
Determines our beliefs, thoughts,
Emotions, and actions
For all of our lives.

Ironically, the second season of our lives
Is the most important in terms of self-determination.
What we choose to do
How we spend our time
Between the ages of 13 and 30
Establishes for the most part
How we spend the balance of our lives
Doing what, with whom.
Best to be wise here
Rather than "old too soon, smart too late." . . .
Our seeds have grown in the daylight.

The third season
Is our productive season.
It is when the heritage and history of our first two seasons
Begin to produce and expand.
It is when the essence of what we are
Personally and professionally
Comes forth and exhibits itself to the world.

It is when the struggle for consistency,
For harmony, for focus, for balance, emerges
As the dance of notes between our genes,
Our environment, our parents, our peers,
Our significant other,
Our work and our play
Seeks the sound of symphony
The resonant chords that are uniquely us.
We here bear the fruit of our seeds and growth.
It is our "rush" of life
Our statement to the world
Which holds the stamps of both approval and affection.

The fourth season
Our final one
Is our harvest
When we reap what we have sown
When what has gone around comes around
When our lives are hopefully better, not bitter.
Our harvest years begin between 55 and 65
And last until we,
Like our forefathers before us,
Collapse back into the earth
Dust into dust
The linear progression of the cycle completed
Our legacy of memories and mementos remaining
And, God willing, the laying to rest of loving good seed.

PULLING IT ALL TOGETHER

The Art of the Trade is to integrate and use the approaches, attitudes, and techniques I have discussed throughout this book. The events in my life—both personal and professional—preceding the sharp, nearly 300-point drop in the Dow Jones Industrials on August 4, 1998, provide an instructive example of how I pulled together a number of the major elements of *The Art of the Trade* to correctly both call and trade on the short side, a significant reversal down in the longest-running bull market in U.S. history.

STALKING A TRADE: SELLING THE U.S. STOCK MARKET SHORT

In terms of demands on my personal and professional life, July 22, 1998, could not have been a worse day for me to stalk a trade, particularly a trade that was shaping up to be a top, and issue a sell signal. But my timing work, specifically my proprietary turning point indicators, had long projected that the last few days of July and/or the first few days of August would be a major turning point time frame for the U.S. stock market.

I began stalking the trade in May 1998. I focused my attention on the U.S. stock market for technical bearish divergences, excessive bullish sentiment, and general fundamental confirmation that a top was close at hand. That's the nice thing about turning points. They specify at what time frames in the future I need to be alert for a significant move in a particular market. In a sense, they put me in the ballpark now for future gain at a precise future date that I know with high probability will be important. The turning points are to me what an experienced guide is to an elk hunter. The guide knows what slope of which mountain, what day, and what time of day he needs to put his elk hunter there if the hunter is to have a chance at harvesting a trophy elk. The turning points do the same for me in the market.

I began mentioning these turning points in the June 11, 1998, issue of my trading newsletter, *The Reaper.* I followed up with more comprehensive discussions in the July 9 and July 23 *Reapers,* which referred specifically to the late July–early August projected turning point. As it turned out, not only did we get a big break in the stock market as projected precisely in this time frame, but on August 7, 1998, the September Japanese yen futures contract again broke to new lows. This renewed pressure on Asian stock markets and currencies was a negative for the U.S. stock market as I saw it. So my turning point work was proved to be valid; it is normally correct 78 to 82 percent of the time (again, Pareto's law: the 80/20 rule).

The challenges that came to me personally and professionally in July preceding this trade were such that they surely gave me an excellent opportunity to "practice what I preach" in this book with regard to markets and trading. I had to maintain my concentration, my focus on the trade, and execute my discipline of "going to work" every day in the markets when there was tremendous chaos and confusion in my personal life and other challenges professionally.

Normally, I live and work by myself. In July, however, prior to the late July–early August turning point, I ended up with six family members in my home, including my elderly mother, who had traveled all the way from Texas to Montana to be with me. You know how family members are—they want to be with you, talk to you, and do things with you. That, of course, is wonderful. That's family, God love 'em. However, all these distractions did take my time and attention away from trading the market. I had to contend with this challenge all of July. Professionally, in addition to researching and writing two issues of my newsletter and recording two daily trading recommendation hotlines, I was under pressure from my publisher to finish this book by the end of the month. I had to work twice the hours that I normally work, amid all the personal chaos surrounding me.

Now, I had been waiting some time for this big opportunity to short the U.S. stock market for a large win. The stealth bear market had already been under way for a while in Asia and Latin America. Moreover, over a third of the stocks traded on the New York Stock Exchange were down 30 percent or more from their highs of the past year and a half, and 71 percent of the stocks on the NASDAQ were down 30 percent or more during that same time period. This was just one of the clues that caused me to suspect that the Dow Jones Industrials rally from June 16 to new highs on July 20 was the last-gasp rally, as well as a false breakout upside. It was, in fact, not confirmed by other stock indices, such as the Russell 2000, Value Line, or the Dow Jones Transports, which did not make new highs.

The challenge for me was staying focused on the task, since I was juggling so many personal and professional balls. Would I be able to harness and integrate my mental faculties to bring them to bear on *The Art of the Trade*—in this case, on shorting the U.S. stock market? Would I exercise the discipline to stay with my homework each and every night prior to the market opening the next morning? Would I follow my own rules of continuing to approach trading as a business? Would I be professional? Would I be able to "steal" enough time for peace and quiet to let the intuition of my right brain harmonize with my left brain's analysis, so that the best of me would be brought to bear on this trade? Or, overwhelmed professionally and personally, would I let my emotions and/or exhaustion get the best of me and cause me to miss this trading opportunity?

As I have discussed earlier in this book, the best trades are the trades that come together slowly, over time, so that when they finally trigger, you can naturally fall into them and flow with them. I had decided in June that the best way to short the U.S. stock market was to short the September Dow Futures Index. The Dow Futures Index contract is a play on the Dow Jones Industrial Average 30 stocks at ten times the index value. Each tick is worth $10, and thus a move, such as a drop from 9000 to 8900 is worth $1000 per contract, or a drop from 9000 to 8500 is worth $5000 per contract. Moreover, the nice thing about this futures contract is that the initial margin where I was trading cost only $3840. (The specifics of this trade can be confirmed by Nell Sloan and Pat Lafferty at Fox Investments in Chicago [800-554-6290] or by Jason or Tammy at Pearce Financial in Destin, FL [800-678-8030].)

READING THE INDICATORS

In addition to my turning point work, where I was projecting a major financial turning point for these markets for the last few trading days in July and/or for the first few trading days in August, market sentiment was too bullish. For weeks on end, well over 80 percent of investors and money managers were overly bullish on stocks, expecting higher prices, thus triggering a contrary opinion sell signal. As I tracked the *Bullish Consensus*'s and *Consensus Magazine*'s bullish sentiment indices for all of 1998, it became overwhelmingly apparent to me that the investing public was excessively bullish on stocks for most of the first half of the year. What alarmed me was that this excessive bullishness ignored the fact the Dow Jones Transports, Value Line, and Russell 2000 had all topped out in April 1998. To me, the DJIA's moving higher was like a motorcyclist going uphill and over a cliff at 100 mph. The biker was still moving forward, still climbing, going higher, but it was only a matter of time until the realities of the law of gravity grabbed him and caused him to plummet. So, too, did I expect the Dow Jones Industrial Average to plummet, following these other indices down from their April highs. This is exactly what occurred. I was right, and it paid off. Indeed, the rally in the Dow Jones Industrial Average from the June 16 low to the July 20 high was a false move, unconfirmed by small cap stocks and the aforementioned indices. Following July 20, the Dow Jones Industrial Average broke sharply to the downside, retracing all the gains made since early March 1998 in a mere 12 trading sessions. Bear markets do occur faster than bull markets! Fear is more powerful than greed. Markets fall of their own weight. When the Dow Jones Industrial Average closed at 8487 on August 4, 1998, it confirmed what is known as a Dow Theory sell signal. In other words, the Dow Jones Industrial Average, by closing below the previous low of 8628 on June 15, came into synchronization with the Dow Jones Transports, which broke the early June three-day-cluster lows on July 29.

Technical confirmation was widely apparent elsewhere. The monthly bar chart of the Dow Jones Industrials indicated that the market had been in an overbought blowoff since mid-1995, the sign of a bubble, a mania (see Figure 10.1). Moreover, the higher prices on the Dow Jones Industrials monthly bar chart were marked by bearish divergence on both the slow stochastic indicator and the relative strength indicator, which were making lower highs as the Dow Jones Industrials were making higher highs on the monthly bar chart. This was a warning sign to look for a market reversal to the downside.

Again, moving from the longer-term perspective toward the shorter one, from the big picture to the small one, the weekly bar chart of the Dow Jones Industrials showed more clearly signs of a market topping (see Figure 10-2). On this weekly bar chart, the Dow Jones Industrials had begun forming a rounded top and, in fact, a double top, since the late first quarter of 1998. Moreover, the moving averages had begun to flatten out and roll over to the downside, with a short-term crossover sell signal. This was another bearish sign. Most important, the lower high on both the slow stochastic indicator and the relative strength indicator when price made a higher high on the Dow Jones Industrials weekly bar chart were clear-cut bearish divergence of two technical indicators from price. Further, the upper end of the channel was clearly being challenged by price on increasingly narrow ranges. The market was struggling to move higher, and weekly trading ranges were increasing to the downside. This was a sign of an approaching top, a trend change to the downside.

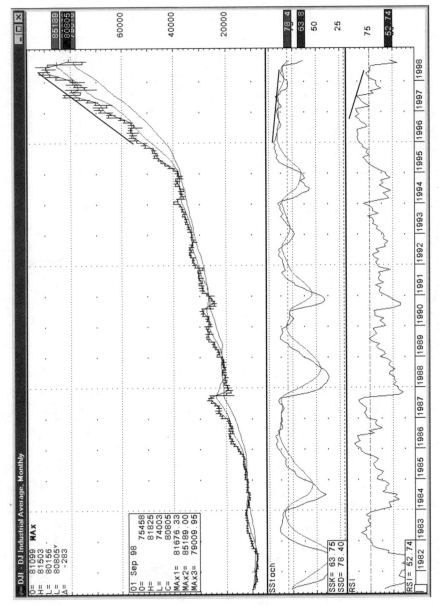

FIGURE 10.1. Dow Jones Industrials—monthly. (Copyright 1998 CQG, Inc.)

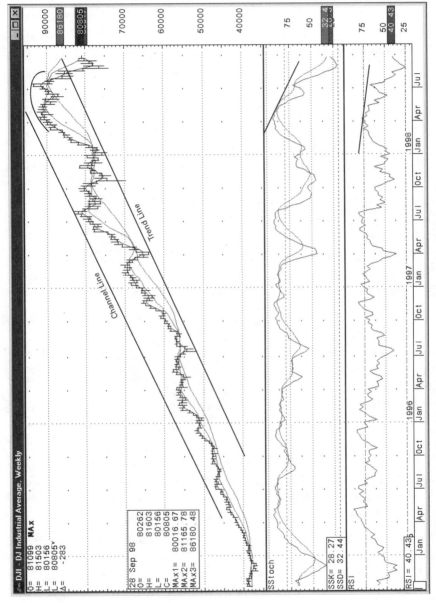

FIGURE 10.2. Dow Jones Industrials—weekly. (Copyright 1998 CQG, Inc.)

To recap, the April top in the Dow Jones Transports and in the Value Line had alerted me to an imminent trend change by the U.S. blue-chip stocks, as represented in the Dow Jones Industrials. The lower highs in July confirmed my thinking. Moving averages had already rolled over to the downside in both the Dow Jones Transports and the Value Line indices (see Figures 10.3 and 10.4).

What surprised me was the third member of the Dow, the Dow Jones Utilities, topping out in June and July (see Figure 10-5). Normally, I would have expected that when the stock market topped out, there would be disintermediation out of stocks into interest-bearing instruments. Investors who place their money in paper assets tend to move from stocks into T-bonds, T-bills, and utilities when a correction and/or a bear market occurs in stocks. This was not the case, however, in utilities. One could, in fact, make the case that the Dow Jones Utilities began topping out in April. So the topping-out process in the Dow Jones Utilities, the distribution, was another technical warning indicator that the Dow Jones Industrials were about to top out and break down.

When price on the Dow Jones Industrials moved to higher highs from July 17 to July 20, and it was not confirmed by the slow stochastic indicator, which made a lower high, I went on red alert to sell short. This created bearish divergence. It was equally confirmed by the slow stochastic indicator on the September Dow Futures Index contract (see Figures 10-6 and 10-7). These dovetailing events helped cement my suspicion that the last rally up to the high on July 20, making new all-time highs, was a false breakout.

Now, I clearly remember what was going on in my personal and professional life in mid- to late July. My elderly mother rightfully needed me—to take her to plays, show her the sights, set off firecrackers, go for rides in the mountains, and play "80" in dominos every evening. Other family members were equally covetous of my time, energy, and efforts. I was being pulled apart. My work station was surrounded by noise, talking, chaos, and confusion, to which I was not accustomed. Remember, I am used to living alone, to peace and quiet. Six people in my house

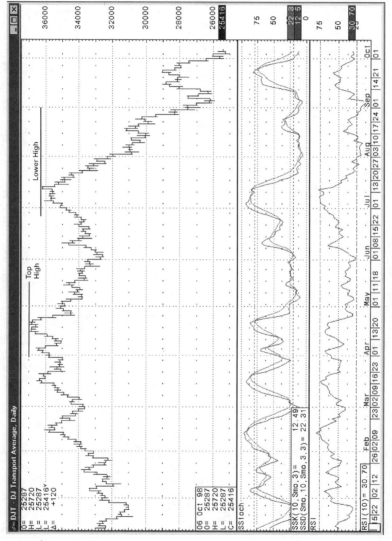

FIGURE 10.3. Dow Jones Transports—daily. (Copyright 1998 CQG, Inc.)

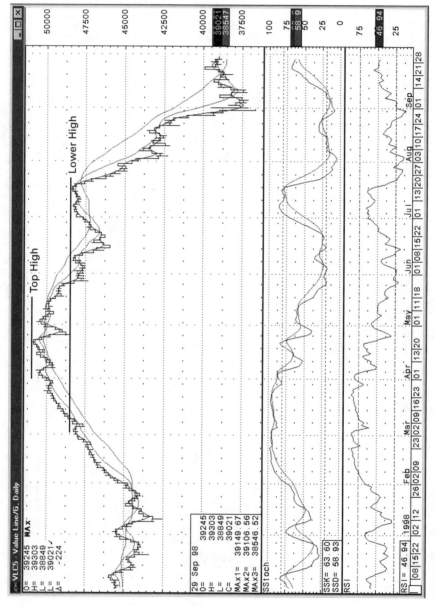

FIGURE 10.4. Value Line—daily. (Copyright 1998 CQG, Inc.)

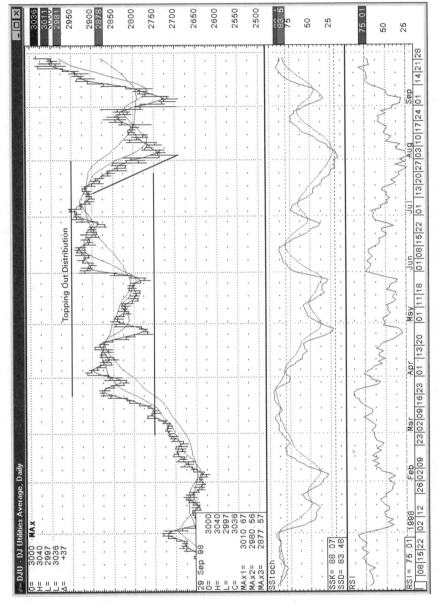

FIGURE 10.5. Dow Jones Utilities—daily. (Copyright 1998 CQG, Inc.)

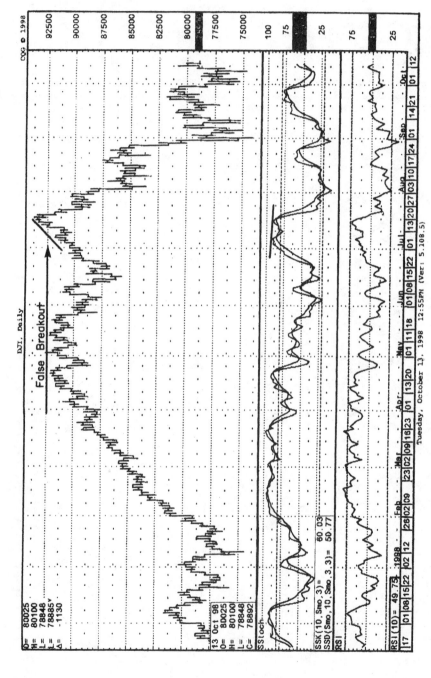

FIGURE 10.6. Dow Jones Industrials—daily. (Copyright 1998 CQG, Inc.)

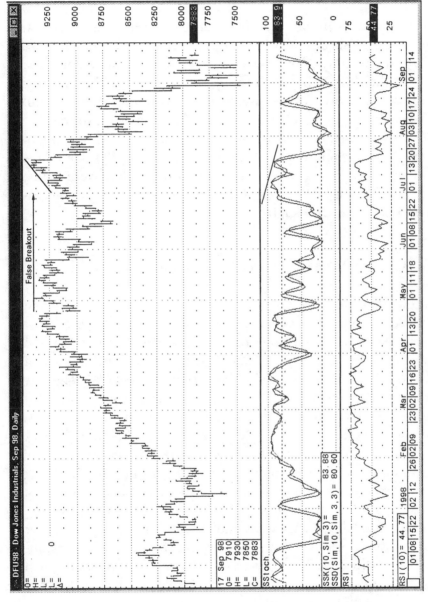

FIGURE 10.7. September Dow Futures Index—daily. (Copyright 1998 CQG, Inc.)

was for me a bit much. Professionally, too, the heat was on—to finish up this book by the end of July, and to prepare a double issue (20 pages) of *The Reaper* by the same date. Talk about a challenge to maintain market trading discipline and focus! It was there, in spades! But I'm happy to report that I pulled it off. I kept the tyranny of the urgent at bay and focused on doing the important things. My well-thought-out and practical trading plan was executed under pressure. Good trading habits minimized the emotional charge of all the pressures and warded off the distractions. It really helped to arise early every morning to prepare for the markets while everyone else was still asleep. This way, the specific market applications of my trading were nailed down before the challenges of the day hit me. It also gave my intuition a chance to kick in.

STICKING WITH THE TRADING SYSTEM

I remember the afternoon and evening of July 21, the day when the Dow Jones Industrials and the Dow Futures Index effectively made an outside day reversal down with a low close. I thought to myself, "This is it. This is the price confirmation of the top that I've been waiting for." I immediately signaled my broker and clients to sell short the September Dow Futures Index for the morning of the next day, July 22—as it turned out, just two days from the high. We took partial profits July 29 to reduce risk in the trade. Then after market consolidation, we again entered the September Dow Futures Index on the short side on the opening the morning of August 4, and caught the huge, nearly 300-point drop that occurred in the Dow Jones Industrials that day, which was equally reflected in the September Dow Futures. On this day alone, we racked up $3620 per contract in profits. We then moved our protective stop losses down in the September Dow Futures Index to 8812 to lock in another guaranteed profit in the trade.

So we entered the market correctly, and then we took partial profits. We reentered again, put our protective stop loss at better than breakeven to ensure at least another small profit, and so we were able to let our remaining profits ride and see if the U.S. stock market, as represented by the September Dow Futures Index, would fall out of bed. We were in a no-risk situation in the hopes of making huge profits over the intermediate to longer term on the downside.

The trading approach that I've put forth in this book was executed professionally, despite the overwhelming personal and other professional challenges. If I can do it, you can do it. How well did I play the game of trading? The odds of the game were in my favor. I found the best business trading opportunity. I did not bet more than I could afford to lose, following my money management principles. I caught the trend change and traded with the new down trend. I played the game correctly and let making money take care of itself. I took partial profits. I was aggressive from studying the lay of the land before I traded. I did the left-brain analytical work and trusted my right-brain intuition. I went contrary to the crowd.

There were no superstitions involved in the trade. All my mental faculties were harnessed and brought to bear upon this short position. I moved my stop to breakeven as soon as possible. I let the market tell me what to do. I stuck with my trading approach. I traded like a rich man, letting the market come to me. I backed into the number of contracts I traded, did my homework the night before, kept track of the trade in my diary, used a proven technical system integrated with my sentiment, timing, and fundamental indicators, worked with good brokers, traded with the style that fits my personality with my customized trading system, paid attention to what was for me glaring fundamental and technical divergences, stalked this trade like a lion stalks its prey, felt the trade flow, and had mastery of my emotions during it. And I was rewarded.

FACTORING IN THE FUNDAMENTALS

I have saved for last in this chapter a "laundry list" of the fundamentals that provided the foundation, supported, and laid the groundwork for this trade. In our day and age, where nearly every trader is a technician, I find that a sound understanding of the market's fundamentals undergirds all other indicators. In the case of the U.S. stock market, the bullish fundamentals were so overwhelming from 1995 into early 1998 that the market went up with only minor consolidations in the face of consistently overbought technical indications on the slow stochastic indicator and relative strength indicator of the monthly bar chart of the Dow Jones Industrials. In other words, from 1995 into 1998, bullish fundamentals so supported the U.S. stock market that they literally invalidated technical, timing, and sentiment indicators.

Beginning with the Asian crisis in July 1997, a shift in fundamentals started to affect the U.S. stock market. This became apparent in 1998. The Asian stock markets, of course, crashed in 1997 and early 1998. Asia represents one-third of the world's economy. It made sense to me that if one-third of the world's economy and stock markets were in crisis, the crash would eventually, inescapably, undermine the U.S. stock market. Also, U.S. corporate exporters would have fewer exports and lower earnings as a result of reduced sales to Asia.

Another fundamental that I found significant leading up to the August 4 break was that U.S. workers, who in 1968 worked 35 hours to buy the equivalent of one share of stock in the S&P Index, in 1998 had to work 88 hours to buy the same share of stock. That made no sense to me. Stocks were way overvalued, not only in terms of this reality but also in terms of dividend yields, and price/earning ratios. Moreover, corporate earnings and growth were unlikely to experience the consistent double-digit levels necessary to sustain excessive market valuations— which, according to my work, placed the market 15 to 30 percent over its worth. The long-term average for the S&P dividend is 3 percent. The S&P dividend yield dropped to less than 1.5 percent in mid-1998. Solid companies normally trade at or slightly over book value, but in mid-1998 the S&P Index was selling for 6.04 times book value. The historical norm for the S&P price/earnings ratio is 14 to 1, but in mid-1998 it stood at a record 28.3 times earnings. Only a quarter of the bull market run in stocks since early 1995 could be attributed to profit growth. Many U.S. stocks in mid-1998 were more expensive than Japanese stocks were when the Japanese Nikkei Dow topped out in 1989.

I also thought it unlikely that U.S. interest rates would fall a full point to cushion any decline in the stock market. Moreover, the failure of corporate interest costs to fall no longer supported Wall Street profits. This meant that interest-sensitive stocks, which make up 40 percent of the New York Stock Exchange, would be pressured. More particularly, why should investors hold U.S. stocks that were moving sideways, not appreciating, and yielding less than 1.5 percent when they could hold U.S. T-bonds with no risk that were yielding more than 5.5 percent? Markets eventually move back to fair value, from being overvalued or undervalued. In addition, since a stealth bear market was taking place in other stock indices such as the Dow Jones Transports, Russell 2000, and Value Line, investors had to be getting nervous. Many of their stocks and some mutual funds had dropped 30 percent or more in value from April through July. Complacency and greed were turning to concern and fear.

Market breadth became poor, leadership was scant, and only a few selective stocks, as well as the blue chips, were moving up. There were more warnings. Historically, megamergers have occurred near the end (at the top) of a bull market. The stock market mutual funds were holding the lowest amount of cash in history. Insiders were continuing to sell stock in the second quarter of 1998. Utilities and some REITs (Real Estate Investment Trusts) started doing relatively better in 1998, indicative of an investor shift in preference of earnings over appreciation. Utilities and REITs normally yield more than most stocks.

The European stock markets were rallying euphorically, in anticipation of the eurocurrency coming onstream in January 1999. That seemed to be an artificial boost to the U.S. stock market. The Russian stock market had fallen 50 percent since May. What happened in Russia would shortly influence Europe and particularly Germany.

The bull market in stocks was featured on the cover of *Time* and *Newsweek*. That's the type of coverage that normally occurs at a top. Children were being taught how to invest in stocks.

This seemed frothy, a bit much. The Bill Clinton–Monica Lewinsky scandal heated up in late July. The U.S. stock market tends to fall when there is uncertainty and falling confidence regarding the sitting president in the White House. Overall, optimism began to fall a bit, as did housing activity. Consumer use of gasoline began to drop off in the peak of the summer driving season, and consumer confidence fell for three straight months.

These are some of the fundamentals that influenced me to look for a bear market in stocks, or at least a stiff correction to the downside.

What if I am wrong? So what? If the stock market bottoms out and then rallies and makes new all-time highs, it won't matter. We've already executed *The Art of the Trade*. We've taken partial profits. It's money in the bank. Our protective stop loss is well below breakeven, thus ensuring at least more partial profits, assuming we don't take additional partial profits before we're stopped out. In short, we're in a situation where, at this point, we cannot lose. And if the market collapses, we can make a fortune, completing the tapestry of *The Art of the Trade*.

FINAL THOUGHTS

The most important lesson I learned personally from writing this book is how important faith is in defeating worry and fear, how critical faith is to preserving psychological capital. Here is how this lesson came about.

I had initially planned to finish this book by the end of May 1998. I did not complete it until August 18, 1998. But, if I had completed the book according to my schedule, instead of God's, some of the most important and powerful information it contains would have been excluded. Specifically, I would not have had Richard Russell's perfect quote from the July 29, 1998, issue of *Dow Theory Letters* at my disposal. At the time Dick Russell penned that quote, he had no idea I was writing a book entitled *The Art of the Trade*. Yet his quote regarding market analysis as an "art," which requires "intuiting" which indicators to use, was ideal to introduce this book. What are the odds of that occurring? Nor did Dick Russell know at the time that I was dedicating this book to him. Neat, huh?

Next, McGraw-Hill/Irwin had originally titled the book *Investing with Both Sides of Your Brain*. On their own, without asking me, they changed the title to *The Art of the Trade*. As it turns out, the title change dovetailed perfectly with what I was writing as well as with the Richard Russell quote. Pretty cool!

Finally, if this book had not been delayed for reasons beyond my control, one of the most important segments—Chapter 10, Pulling It All Together—would not have been included. The all-important stock market sell signal and trade, how it evolved and developed, did not occur until late July and early August 1998. Chapter 10, in my opinion, is crucial in tying the whole book together.

What are the odds of all these perfectly dovetailing harmonious events occurring independently, without the knowledge and contrary to the will of the separate parties? The probabilities are off the scale. I consider such off-the-scale probabilities to be minor miracles—not parting the Red Sea or water-into-wine miracles, but nevertheless the active acts of God in our lives. So we do "walk by faith, not by sight." And when we have the faith to so walk, we are at peace, become more fully conscious, and preserve our precious psychological capital.

QUESTIONS AND ANSWERS

1. **Would you give some specific examples of how your perspective on the importance of the long-term view, on doing what is important and not urgent, applies to the markets?**

   In trading, this means undergoing the short-term pain of buying on weakness, when the market is declining in the short run, buying at support on the up trendline on the weekly chart in anticipation of a continuation of the up move.

   Another example in futures is to look first at the monthly continuation bar charts, then the weekly continuation bar charts, then the daily bar charts, and finally the intraday charts in order to reach a trading decision. In other words, I go from the longer-term perspective to the shorter-term perspective in implementing a trading decision. The monthly and weekly bar charts give me the overview and trend of the market and the daily and intraday charts help me time my entry into the market more effectively.

   If you look at the charts in the reverse order, checking the intraday and daily bar charts first, it's like looking at trees before you have the view of what the forest is all about. You lose your perspective, get wrapped up in all the little details, and get off track with regard to your long-term goals and objectives. Similarly, when you're analyzing the markets over the short term, you tend to miss the expanded view of where a market is going by way of a bigger move and the major trend. Usually, a short-term view, the tyranny of the urgent, unproductive emotion, and chaos run together, whereas a long-term view, the important things in life, a sense of logical, ordered priorities, and organization run together.

2. **How important is a broker in your trading philosophy?**

I consider a broker to be very important. A broker is part of your team, part of your mindfield, if you will. But just as it's easier to get along with a spouse who is like-minded, so is it easier to flow with a broker who is like-minded, who shares your trading approach and philosophy, and who is in tune with what you're attempting to do. The relationship enhances your psychological capital. A competent broker also provides insight, research, and information you wouldn't have otherwise. A good team approach is better than an individual approach. By myself, I cannot outfight Mike Tyson, but I guarantee that with six other guys together all at the same time, we have a fighting chance of subduing him.

Other important considerations include having a broker who is sympathetic and who provides you with the information you need as well as reasonable round-turn commission costs. It may be cheaper to trade online without a broker, but then you trade alone, and your trades will actually take longer to execute.

3. **From your writings, I get the sense that flow is very important to you, that you are not a great believer in frantic day-trading activity. Is this true?**

Yes. I think the high intensity and emotional overload of day trading quickly burn out psychological capital and are detrimental long term to physical health and financial well-being. So I like to wait for my trades. To achieve a sense of flow, your trading should not come across as a jumbled struggle. You should feel like you're driving on a smooth, newly paved highway, not an unpaved, pothole-infested mountain road.

Overtrading and day trading can kill that sense of flow. Also, I don't believe you should have more positions in the market than you can comfortably follow. It creates too much stress on your psychological and financial capital. You need to stay within your comfort level and sell down to your sleeping level, which means literally not having more positions on than you can sleep with. Day trading is okay occasionally. Overtrading and day trading off the floor are the hallmarks of action seekers, to my way of thinking. Some become desperate. Desperate people do desperate things and seldom succeed at them.

Here are some tips to help achieve the best flow in your trading results:

- Be patient and wait for the trades to develop.
- Spread your risk among various markets, but don't trade too many markets at the same time.

- Remain aware of the technical, psychological, timing, and fundamental aspects of each market. Recognize that all markets and trades are somewhat different and have unique characteristics, so trade them accordingly.

- Have the patience to stay out of the market when you don't understand it, when you're sick, when you're truly troubled, or when you're thoroughly distracted.

- Trade consistent with your emotional profile, whether it is swing trading, trading with the trend, buying or selling resistance in the trading range, or playing options.

- Practice good money management. Look to break even as soon as possible, even if that means taking partial profits. At the same time, attempt to trade with the trend and let your profits ride and cut your losses short.

- Be satisfied. Know that the odds are that you will not be able to buy at the bottom and sell at the top. Settle for a piece of the middle.

- Watch market consensus and volume. Be cautious about buying in a market when better than 80 percent are bullish. Be reluctant to sell in a market when over 80 percent are bearish. Monitor volume, and trade healthy markets that show increasing volume. Look for lack of volume or extreme volume at tops and bottoms. See if that volume activity is coupled with extreme bullish or extreme bearish sentiment.

- Fine-tune your trading plan, but generally stick with the same plan over time if it's proven. Make only small adjustments as long as you are successful.

- Be careful to guard against greed or fear, and never trade with money that's vital to the welfare of your family. Be sure you have plenty of risk capital to use for trading. A 20 percent buffer is good to have on hand.

- Let a market trade play itself out according to your original plan. Be reluctant to jump in and out of a trade before it has a chance to develop and mature.

4. **Is it correct that trading the markets is a continual learning process that requires some adjustment?**

Yes. This is why you should paper-trade your system before you put your money on the line in the markets. Then you should start slowly, trading a small amount of money and a few contracts or shares to integrate your personal emotional idiosyncrasies into trading. Clean up your act before trading big money. In other words, make sure your business works well first on paper. Then start with small amounts of money and learn your weaknesses and limits before you put large amounts of psychological and financial capital on the line in the trading pits.

In a sense, you could view yourself as being "rusty." You have to fine-tune your skills, just as a football team has to go through preseason training and games before putting it all on the line during the regular season. This means you must have patience and humility to learn from your mistakes and correct them. We often grow only after we make a mistake and learn from it. As you increase your pool of knowledge in your left brain and become quiet and relaxed—confident, comfortable, competent, and capable—you can let intuition take over in your right brain and let the lower brain frequencies move you quickly along to being an excellent trader.

Remember, the goal is excellence, not perfection. It all begins with having the humility and patience to be a student, to build your base of knowledge, a foundation from which you will continue to grow.

5. **You've talked about similarities between trading and gambling. Does trading have anything in common with playing chess?**

Yes. Good chess players are able to think about their position, strategy, tactics, and moves five to six sequences ahead. Good chess players are also able to analyze and discern their opponent's strategy, tactics, and potential moves five to six moves into the future. In like manner, good traders will look at both sides of the market, and will attempt to understand both the bull's and the bear's case thoroughly before taking a position. Traders, too, will take a long-term view.

6. **As I understand it, all of us have to stand on our own two feet with regard to trading decisions. At the same time, you talk about how none of us is an island and that we need other people. How do you balance this view in your personal trading?**

The buck stops here. I take personal responsibility and make the final decision on all my trading approaches. I am CEO and president of my own small trading firm. At the same time, I surround myself with people who are like-minded and supportive, and who add value to my life as I add value to theirs. They do research and provide other types of support that enhance my trading effort. This is the balance, as I see it, between the individual and the group in trading.

7. Do you pay much attention to what is written about or said in the financial media?

Yes, I do. The financial media—including television, radio, the Internet, financial newsletters, magazines, and newspapers—provide fundamentally important financial input. They give me a public perspective on the markets, as well as insight about the economic environment in which we all exist and hope to prosper. But I look for extremes in media opinion that may alert me to an acceleration of the present trend in the market (20 percent probability) or a trend reversal (80 percent probability). I also pay attention when a market doesn't do what the general consensus expects it to do. This is often a big red warning flag of an upcoming trend change.

8. What do you think is the greatest pitfall to being a successful trader?

I think too many traders come to the trading arena expecting to find the Holy Grail, to get rich quickly. The vast majority miss the perspective that the key to being successful is to do the work themselves and execute the solid, proven principles of trading that also apply to a small business. Trading is an art as well as a science. It requires both a right-brain and a left-brain approach. In fact, it can be argued that to be successful in trading long term is the most difficult occupation there is. This is because trading requires you to have your personal act together as well as to be professional, capable, competent, and consistent. There is no substitute for knowing yourself, for having a well-developed trading approach and business plan, and for developing the flexibility, patience, responsibility, and humility to make the necessary adjustments. A key is to get rich slowly and be content with it.

9. What is so wrong about missing a trade, if a trade is like a bus that comes by every 15 minutes?

There are opportunity costs and there are opportunities lost. Put differently, yes, you can lose money when you enter a trade and it is unsuccessful, when you are stopped out. When you pass on a winning trade because you were afraid of being wrong, you were lazy, or you chose instead to go fishing, it is an opportunity lost. The losses, although not registered in your trading account, are just as real as if you were in a trade and had been stopped out of it.

Let the bus (trade) go by, however, when you're in a traumatized state—for example, after the death of a close family member, a major car accident, or a serious illness—or when you're already loaded up with positions and you can't sleep well.

10. How much does luck have to do with trading?

We live in an imperfect world with imperfect and incomplete information. So when you put your money on the line, you do so in an environment of uncertainty. In a sense, your fate is in the hands of God and is somewhat subject to luck.

More important, you must realize that the market is neutral emotionally when it comes to you. Some traders fear success as much as others fear failure. The market doesn't punish you. It doesn't give you money or deny you money. Many traders need to deal with the fact that their hangups in trading have to do with what they're willing to give or deny themselves, and how they subjectively perceive and respond to reality (the market). This is directly related to how good they feel about themselves. If you feel good about yourself, you generally feel you deserve what you earn. Then you will find that you have a much better chance of approaching the market in a way that allows it to reward you. Some people just can't handle too much success. They self-destruct. They feel unworthy to receive what they are making in the market.

11. Do you ever trade on tips, on recommendations coming from a fellow trader?

Yes. I have successful partners with whom I have consistently made money. When it comes to a tip or a trade recommendation in the market, I look at the source and see if I consider it trustworthy and professional. I make sure my source has the character, professionalism, reliability, and track record that I can rely on. It also helps if the source has more money on the line in the trade than I do. Then I further analyze the trade as best I can. If it stands on its own merit, I will take the trading tip.

Keep in mind that if you buy on Paul's advice, you must sell on Paul's advice. Listen on both ends. Don't take half of someone's advice. You have to assume that if a person offering a tip knows that much about when to get in, he or she will also know when to get out. If you're going to let people quarterback you, let them be the quarterback, call the plays, and run the team, so to speak. Obviously, if they recommend something flagrantly absurd, don't stick around. But as long as the advice is reasonable, consistent, and professional, fine.

12. How do you handle attacks on your trading position? What do you do when someone builds a case and attempts to prove that your trading position is "wrong"?

    I listen respectfully and then analyze the arguments to see if any of them have merit with regard to my position. If they do, I make an appropriate adjustment. But I tend to give my original thinking the benefit of the doubt. Keep in mind that much of what you hear from the financial media and other traders is simply propaganda, or old news, long ago discounted by the market. Either it's untrue (or of marginal use) or the market has already discounted it.

13. Do you ever add to a losing position or average down?

    I don't consider this to be a sound trading practice. It violates my original trading plan. It is based on hope, rather than on responding realistically to what the market is doing. When you find yourself hoping, you are in danger of taking a large loss and should exit the trade. We all have a tendency to believe what we want. We interpret events in line with what we want to believe, rather than what is true. We prefer to see and hear what is pleasant and comfortable to us. But either we line up with the market or we lose.

14. Which is the stronger emotion, fear or greed?

    Fear. This is why markets go down three times faster than they go up.

15. Can you ever put fear to good use?

    Yes, you can. When you sweat entering a trade, when you fear your decision may not be the correct one, it's often the best time to enter the trade, particularly if you've done your homework, the trade makes logical sense, and your intuition says, "Go." You're in status quo humility. When you have limited information, you're in that environment of uncertainty, so you have to sweat it out a bit. There's no reward without risk. The best trade is usually one that concerns you because it's such a new move, it hasn't been discounted by the market yet. Typically, this occurs when you're buying in the bottom third of a new move up. There is little fundamental information to support your position.

    On the other hand, when you are complacent with the trade because you have fat profits, or you hope the market is going to go higher to increase your profits, you ought to consider taking some of the profits down and banking them. Also, when you find yourself being greedy, you should consider taking at least partial profits instead of adding to your position.

16. **What leads to so many traders taking small profits while incurring large losses?**

It is the unwillingness to accept defeat and admit to faulty judgment. This is due to pride of opinion. They don't want to be wrong.

17. **When making a trading decision, how much weight do you assign to technical, timing, sentiment, and fundamental indicators?**

You have to have an intuitive and experiential sense of what to use and what to throw out. Obviously, if the market is trending, you use different technical tools than if it's swinging or in a trading range. How to balance out fundamental, technical, sentiment, and timing indicators will differ from trade to trade and market to market.

If the markets continue to move and violate sentiment, technical, and timing indicators, because the fundamentals are so powerful that they override all else, you are best served by not listening to any other signals. This was the case when negative economic fundamentals were the overriding force on the Japanese yen bear market in 1996, 1997, and 1998. The U.S. stock market on the upside during these same years was influenced by the overriding fundamentals of money flowing into the U.S. economy from Europe and Asia; also Americans were viewing the stock market as a place to save, plunking $20 to $30 million a month into stock mutual funds, which had to invest that money. These factors overrode and invalidated any excessive bullishness, cycles and turning points, and technical overbought conditions. It paid to ignore the technical sell signals. This is the essence of *The Art of the Trade*.

GLOSSARY

bearish divergence   When technical indicators deviate from price and fail to confirm a price up trend. The reverse is true in a down trend.

crossover signal   A buy or sell signal issued when a smaller moving average (like a 3-day) crosses a longer-term moving average (like a 9-day).

day trading   Frequent, daily trading in and out of the markets, possibly from 5 to 20 times a day.

entry point   A market price at which a trading system triggers a buy or sell signal.

investing   Investors buy and sell for the long term. They look for stocks, bonds, currencies, and commodities that are undervalued, and hold these investments for appreciation and dividends (in the case of stocks).

limit move   The maximum amount a futures contract can trade higher or lower on a given trading day.

long   A trading position that increases in value as the market rallies and decreases in value as the market declines.

margin   The amount of money (sometimes as little as 5 percent) required to be put on deposit with a broker in order to establish a specific leveraged market position.

margin account   Money traders must set aside to cover establishing initial positions in the market and to cover potential losses. Traders are wise to keep this excess money and money used for initial margin invested in Treasury bills earning interest or other money market funds.

margin call   Notification from a broker of insufficient money in a trading account to cover the positions a trader has established in the market, usually because the market has moved against the trader's positions.

margin capital   The initial amount of money held in a margin account, used to leverage trades.

market support   The recent or historical price level that has sparked buying in the past; the point where buyers expect prices to bottom.

money management   The allocation of personal financial assets in three steps. First traders must decide how much capital they're willing to trade with in their account. Then they must decide how much they're willing to trade in any particular market sector. Last, they must decide how much they are willing to risk on any individual trade.

moving-average investing   Buying or selling a market on the basis of a crossover buy or sell signal, such as a 3-day moving average crossing above (buy) or below (sell) a 9-day moving average.

open interest   The number of people involved in the market on both the long and short side of a futures contract. This is often a good indication of liquidity, how large a trading position a trader can have in a market, and whether a trader can expect reasonable executions on entries and exits. Open interest tells traders if the odds are good that, whenever they want to get in or out of a trade, they'll be forced to feed positions into the market slowly, a little at a time, or be able to get out all at once. This is similar to looking at the number of a company's shares outstanding in the stock market. You want liquidity in the markets. Open interest is to be used in conjunction with volume, the number of contracts traded on a particular day.

point and figure   A technical method of market price analysis using boxes with X's and O's, ignoring time.

resistance   The recent or historical price level that has sparked selling in the past; the point where sellers expect a ceiling on a market price advance.

scale down   Buying on a systematic basis as prices fall (also called *averaging down*).

scale up   Selling on a systematic basis as prices rise (also called *averaging up*).

setup   A confluence of technical signals that in combination trigger buy or sell signals.

short   A trading position that increases in value as the market declines and decreases in value as the market rallies.

spread   A trade between two related, tradable markets to exploit the relative difference in price, looking for the spread to expand or contract. Or a combination of futures or options positions in which the trader is both the buyer and the seller of the same type of instrument on the same underlying stock or commodity, with the instruments having different exercise prices or expiration dates.

stop (buy or sell)   A buy stop is an order placed at a predetermined price over the current price of the market; that price, when hit, triggers a market order entry into the trade. A sell stop is an order placed at a predetermined price below the current market price; that price, when hit, triggers a market order entry into the trade.

stop loss A risk management technique in which the trade is liquidated to halt any further decline in value on a long position once the market price has fallen to a specific level, triggering the protective stop loss and sell order. Works in reverse for short positions.

straddle Purchase or sale of an equivalent number of puts and calls on an underlying stock with the same exercise price and expiration date, used to hedge against potential losses, whichever way the market moves. Also used in sophisticated commodity trading. A straddle buyer expects that the price of the stock or commodity will soon break out of its trading range, whereas a straddle writer is betting on little change in the price of the underlying stock or commodity during the life of the futures or options contract.

strike price The price per unit at which the holder of an option may receive or deliver the underlying unit; also known as the *exercise price.*

support Historical price level at which falling prices have stopped falling and either moved sideways or reversed direction; can be seen as a price chart pattern.

swing trading Focusing on short-term to intermediate-term breakout moves, or springboard setups, where a trader can gather profits in a couple of days to a few weeks in a directional price move.

swings Measurement of price movement of a tradable market between extreme highs and lows, or lows and highs.

technical analysis A form of market analysis that predicts price movement for securities and commodities solely on the basis of technical indicators gleaned from market price action. This method ignores fundamental, sentiment, and time studies.

technical setup When a number of technical indicators coincide to complement each other in triggering a buy or sell signal.

tick Minimum fluctuation of a tradable market. For example, bonds trade in thirty-seconds, whereas most stocks trade in eighths.

trading A subset of investing. Traders may look for anomalies in the market that provide opportunities for profit. They may buy the same securities or commodities that investors buy, but they normally won't hold them as long. Traders also approach the market from the short side, whereas investors don't sell short.

trend trading Trading in harmony with a market's price trend. For example, using a moving-average approach to trading with the trend.

volume The level of trading in a market on a particular day. Volume is the pulse, the lifeblood, of the market, indicating how many people have come to the party. If a trader is trend or swing trading and prices are going up on increasing volume, it's a healthy market. Then, if volume spikes higher, the market may be near exhaustion. If the price continues to rise sluggishly on low or falling volume, this may also indicate the top of the market.

When a market is going down, a trader who is on the short side wants the price drop to occur on increasing volume. A huge spike in volume, though, may indicate exhaustion in selling. Or, if volume drops off significantly and dries up, with sluggish price movement, the market may be close to a trading bottom.

BIBLIOGRAPHY

Becker, Dr. Robert O., Gary Seldon, and Maria Guamaschelli. *The Body Electric: Electromagnetism and the Foundation of Life.* William Morrow, 1987.

Becker, Dr. Robert O., Gary Seldon, and Maria Guamaschelli. *Cross Currents: The Promise of Electromedicine, the Perils of Electropollution.* J. P. Tarcher, 1991.

Browne, Harry. *Harry Browne Special Reports: 16 Golden Rules for Financial Safety.* 1997, pp. 191–214.

Burr, Dr. Harold Saxton, M.D. *Blueprint for Immortality: The Electric Patterns of Life.* N. Spearman, 1986.

Callahan, Phillip S. *Tuning In to Nature: Solar Energy, Infrared Radiation, and the Insect Communication System.* Devin-Adair Company, 1975.

Covey, Stephen R. *The Seven Habits of Highly Successful People.* Simon and Schuster, 1990.

Davis, Dick. *Dick Davis Digest,* April 1998.

Drucker, Dr. Peter. *The Executive in Action: Managing for Results, Innovation, and Entrepreneurship—The Effective Executive.* Harper Business, 1996.

Edwards, Robert D., and John. R. Magee. *Technical Analysis of Stock Trends.* AMACOM Books, 1997.

Fisher, Kenneth L. *One Hundred Minds That Make the Market.* Business Classics, 1994.

Grant, James. *Bernard M. Baruch: The Adventures of a Wall Street Legend.* John Wiley & Sons, 1997.

Hill, John. *Scientific Interpretation of Bar Charts.* Commodity Research, 1979.

Hill, Napoleon. *Think and Grow Rich.* Ballantine Books, 1996.

Hunt, Dr. Valerie. *Infinite Mind.* Malibu Publishing, 1996.

Keleman, Stanley. *Your Body Speaks Its Mind: The Bioenergetic Way to Greater Emotional and Sexual Satisfaction,* Center Press, 1981.

Levine, Mark, and Stephen M. Pollan. *Die Broke: A Radical, Four-Part Financial Plan to Restore Your Confidence, Increase Your Net Worth, and Afford You the Lifestyle of Your Dreams.* Harper Business, 1997.

McMaster, R. E., Jr. *The Christ Within: The Church and New Age Seek Him.* A.N. Inc. International, 1995.

McMaster, R. E., Jr. *A Highlander's Passion,* Mountain Spring Press, 1997.

Niederhoffer, Victor. *The Education of a Speculator.* John Wiley & Sons, 1998.

Peters, Tom. *Liberation Management: Necessary Disorganization for the Nanosecond Nineties.* Knopf, 1992.

Rush, Martin, M.D. *Bottom Line,* August 1, 1998.

Ryce, Dr. Michael. *Why Is This Happening to Me Again?!* ISBN 1-886562-29-6, 1997.

Stanley, Thomas. *The Millionaire Next Door.* Longstreet, 1996.

Staton, Mary Tunstall. *The Staton Institute Advisory,* March 1998.

INDEX

ABOUT THE AUTHOR

R. E. McMaster, an accomplished and successful trader for over 25 years, is an investment consultant with clients in more than 40 countries. He is editor and publisher of *The Reaper,* an international financial, economic, and investment newsletter with a global readership of 50,000. Featured in *Unconventional Wisdom* as one of 12 remarkable innovators, McMaster previously worked as a top money manager with E.F. Hutton and was a U.S. Air Force pilot. His success, experience, and knowledge make McMaster a popular speaker at conferences and seminars around the world.

Mr. McMaster is the author of the following books: *Cycles of War: The Next Six Years, The Trader's Notebook (1978), The Traders's Notebook (1979), The Trader's Notebook (1980), Wealth for All: Religion, Politics and War, Wealth for All: Economics, No Time for Slaves, McMaster's Eight M's of Successful Investing, The Power of Total Perspective, The Christ Within,* and *A Highlander's Passion (Heartfelt Poetry).*